CHICAGO PUBLIC LIBRARY
P9-CLC-063

Chicago Public Library
C
P
L
REFERENCE
Form 178 rev. 11-00

career ideas for teens in the arts and communications

Diane Lindsey Reeves
with Gail Karlitz and Don Rauf

Ferguson
An imprint of Facts On File

Career Ideas for Teens in the Arts and Communications

Ferguson
An imprint of Facts On File, Inc.
132 West 31st Street
New York NY 10001

Library of Congress Cataloging-in-Publication Data

Reeves, Diane Lindsey, 1959–
Career ideas for teens in the arts and communications / Diane Lindsey Reeves with Gail Karlitz and Don Rauf.
p. cm.
Includes index.
ISBN 0-8160-5288-3 (hc: alk. paper)
1. Arts—Vocational guidance—Juvenile literature. I. Karlitz, Gail. II. Rauf, Don. III. Title.
NX163.R44 2005
700'.23'73—dc22

2004008437

Ferguson books are available at special discounts when purchased in bulk quantities for businesses, associations, institutions, or sales promotions. Please call our Special Sales Department in New York at (212) 967-8800 or (800) 322-8755.

You can find Ferguson on the World Wide Web at http://www.fergpubco.com

Text design by Joel and Sandy Armstrong
Cover design by Nora Wertz
Illustrations by Matt Wood

Printed in the United States of America

VB PKG 10 9 8 7 6 5 4 3 2 1

This book is printed on acid-free paper.

contents

acknowledgments

A million thanks to the people who took the time to share their career stories and provide photos for this book:

Steven Bleicher
Stuart Brooks
Trish Burgio
Barbara Davis-Long
Jessica Douglas
Stacey Freed
Robert Goodman
Jay Jennings
Lela Katzman
Kevin Kiernan
Mildred Lang
Jena McGregor
Konica Mendez
Traci Mosser
Ovi Nedelu
Doug Van De Zande
Lyle Welden
Joyce Wiswell

And a big thank-you to our project interns and research assistants:

Susannah Driver
Lindsey Reeves

career ideas for teens

welcome to your future

Q: What's one of the most boring questions adults ask teens?

A: "So . . . what do you want to be when you grow up?"

Well-meaning adults always seem so interested in what you plan to be.

You, on the other hand, are just trying to make it through high school in one piece.

But you may still have a nagging feeling that you really need to find some direction and think about what you want to do with your life.

When it comes to choosing your life's work there's some good news and some bad news. The good news is that, according to the U.S. Bureau of Labor Statistics, you have more than 12,000 different occupations to choose from. With that many options there's got to be something that's just right for you.

Right?

Absolutely.

But . . .

Here comes the bad news.

THERE ARE MORE THAN 12,000 DIFFERENT OCCUPATIONS TO CHOOSE FROM!

How in the world are you ever going to figure out which one is right for you?

We're so glad you asked!

Helping high school students like you make informed choices about their future is what this book (and each of the other titles in the *Career Ideas for Teens* series) is all about. Here you'll encounter 10 tough questions designed to help you answer the biggest one of all: "What in the world am I going to do after I graduate from high school?"

The *Career Ideas for Teens* series enables you to expand your horizons beyond the "doctor, teacher, lawyer" responses common to those new to the career exploration process. The books provide a no-pressure introduction to real jobs that real people do. And they offer a chance to "try on" different career options before committing to a specific college program or career path. Each title in this series is based on one of the 16 career clusters established by the U.S. Department of Education.

And what is a career cluster, you ask? Career clusters are based on a simple and very useful concept. Each cluster consists of all entry-level through professional-level occupations in a broad industry area. All of the jobs and industries in a cluster have many things in common. This organizational structure makes it easier for people like you to get a handle on the big world of work. So instead of rushing headlong into a mind-boggling exploration of the entire universe of career opportunities, you get a chance to tiptoe into smaller, more manageable segments first.

We've used this career cluster concept to organize the *Career Ideas for Teens* series of books. For example, careers related to the arts, communication, and entertainment are organized or "clustered" into the *Career Ideas for Teens in the Arts and Communications* title; a wide variety of health care professions are included in *Career Ideas for Teens in Health Science*; and so on.

Clueless as to what some of these industries are all about? Can't even imagine how something like manufacturing or public administration could possibly relate to you?

No problem.

You're about to find out. Just be prepared to expect the unexpected as you venture out into the world of work. There are some pretty incredible options out there, and some pretty surprising ones too. In fact, it's quite possible that you'll discover that the ideal career for you is one you had never heard of before.

Whatever you do, don't cut yourself short by limiting yourself to just one book in the series. You may find that your initial interests guide you towards the health sciences field—which would, of course, be a good place to start. However, you may discover some new "twists" with a look through the arts and communications book. There you may find a way to blend your medical interests with your exceptional writing and speaking skills by considering becoming a public relations (PR) specialist for a hospital or pharmaceutical company. Or look at the book on education to see about becoming a public health educator or school nurse.

Before you get started, you should know that this book is divided into three sections, each representing an important step toward figuring out what to do with your life.

The first eight titles in the *Career Ideas for Teens* series focus on:

- Architecture and Construction
- Arts and Communications
- Education and Training
- Government and Public Service
- Health Science
- Information Technology
- Law and Public Safety
- Manufacturing

Before You Get Started

Unlike most books, this one is meant to be actively experienced, rather than merely read. Passive perusal won't cut it. Energetic engagement is what it takes to figure out something as important as the rest of your life.

As we've already mentioned, you'll encounter 10 important questions as you work your way through this book. Following each Big Question is an activity designated with a symbol that looks like this:

Every time you see this symbol, you'll know it's time to invest a little energy in your future by getting out your notebook or binder, a pen or pencil, and doing whatever the instructions direct you to do. If this book is your personal property, you can choose to do the activities right in the book. But you still might want to make copies of your finished products to go in a binder so they are all in one place for easy reference.

When you've completed all the activities, you'll have your own personal **Big Question AnswerBook**, a planning guide representing a straightforward and truly effective process you can use throughout your life to make fully informed career decisions.

discover you at work

This first section focuses on a very important subject: You. It poses four Big Questions that are designed specifically to help you "discover you":

? Big Question #1: **who are you?**
? Big Question #2: **what are your interests and strengths?**
? Big Question #3: **what are your work values?**

Then, using an interest assessment tool developed by the U.S. Department of Labor and implemented with your very vivid imagination, you'll picture yourself doing some of the things that people actually do for their jobs. In other words, you'll start "discovering you at work" by answering the following:

? Big Question #4: **what's your work personality?**

Unfortunately, this first step is often a misstep for many people. Or make that a "missed" step. When you talk with the adults in your life about their career choices, you're likely to find that some of them never even considered the idea of choosing a career based on personal preferences and strengths. You're also likely to learn that if they had it to do over again, this step would definitely play a significant role in the choices they would make.

explore your options

There's more than meets the eye when it comes to finding the best career to pursue. There are also countless ways to blend talent or passion in these areas in some rather unexpected and exciting ways. Get ready to find answers to two more Big Questions as you browse through an entire section of career profiles:

? Big Question #5: **do you have the right skills?**
? Big Question #6: **are you on the right path?**

experiment with success

At long last you're ready to give this thing called career planning a trial run. Here's where you'll encounter three Big Questions that will unleash critical decision-making strategies and skills that will serve you well throughout a lifetime of career success.

While you're at it, take some time to sit in on a roundtable discussion with successful professionals representing a very impressive array of careers related to this industry. Many of their experiences will apply to your own life, even if you don't plan to pursue the same careers.

? Big Question #7: **who knows what you need to know?**
? Big Question #8: **how can you find out what a career is really like?**
? Big Question #9: **how do you know when you've made the right choice?**

Then as you begin to pull all your new insights and ideas together, you'll come to one final question:

? Big Question #10: **what's next?**

As you get ready to take the plunge, remember that this is a book about possibilities and potential. You can use it to make the most of your future work!

Here's what you'll need to complete the Big Question AnswerBook:

- A notebook or binder for the completed activities included in all three sections of the book
- An openness to new ideas
- Complete and completely candid answers to the 10 Big Question activities

So don't just read it, do it.
Plan it.
Dream it.

SECTION 1 discover you at work

The goal here is to get some clues about who you are and what you should do with your life. As time goes by, you will grow older, become more educated, and have more experiences, but many things that truly define you are not likely to change. Even now you possess very strong characteristics—genuine qualities that mark you as the unique and gifted person that you undoubtedly are.

It's impossible to overestimate the importance of giving your wholehearted attention to this step. You, after all, are the most valuable commodity you'll ever have to offer a future employer. Finding work that makes the most of your assets often means the difference between enjoying a rewarding career and simply earning a paycheck.

You've probably already experienced the satisfaction of a good day's work. You know what we mean—those days when you get all your assignments in on time, you're prepared for the pop quiz your teacher sprung on you, and you beat your best time during sports practice. You may be exhausted at the end of the day but you can't help but feel good about yourself and your accomplishments. A well-chosen career can provide that same sense of satisfaction. Since you're likely to spend upwards of 40 years doing some kind of work, well-informed choices make a lot of sense!

Let's take a little time for you to understand yourself and connect what you discover about yourself to the world of work.

To find a career path that's right for you, we'll tackle these three Big Questions first:

- **who are you?**
- **what are your interests and strengths?**
- **what are your work values?**

Big Question #1: who are you?

Have you ever noticed how quickly new students in your school or new families in your community find the people who are most like them? If you've ever been the "new" person yourself, you've probably spent your first few days sizing up the general population and then getting in with the people who dress in clothes a lot like yours, appreciate the same style of music, or maybe even root for the same sports teams.

Given that this process happens so naturally—if not necessarily on purpose—it should come as no surprise that many people lean toward jobs that surround them with people most like them. When people with common interests, common values, and complementary talents come together in the workplace, the results can be quite remarkable.

Many career aptitude tests, including the one developed by the U.S. Department of Labor and included later in this book, are based on the theory that certain types of people do better at certain types of jobs. It's like a really sophisticated matchmaking service. Take your basic strengths and interests and match them to the strengths and interests required by specific occupations.

It makes sense when you think about it. When you want to find a career that's ideally suited for you, find out what people like you are doing and head off in that direction!

There's just one little catch.

The only way to recognize other people like you is to recognize yourself. Who are you anyway? What are you like? What's your basic approach to life and work?

Now's as good a time as any to find out. Let's start by looking at who you are in a systematic way. This process will ultimately help you understand how to identify personally appropriate career options.

Big Activity #1:
who are you?

On a sheet of paper, if this book doesn't belong to you, create a list of adjectives that best describe you. You should be able to come up with at least 15 qualities that apply to you. There's no need to make judgments about whether these qualities are good or bad. They just are. They represent who you are and can help you understand what you bring to the workforce.

(If you get stuck, ask a trusted friend or adult to help describe especially strong traits they see in you.)

Some of the types of qualities you may choose to include are:

- **How you relate to others:**
  Are you shy? Outgoing? Helpful? Dependent? Empathic? In charge? Agreeable? Challenging? Persuasive? Popular? Impatient? A loner?
- **How you approach new situations:**
  Are you adventurous? Traditional? Cautious? Enthusiastic? Curious?
- **How you feel about change—planned or unplanned:**
  Are you resistant? Adaptable? Flexible? Predictable?
- **How you approach problems:**
  Are you persistent? Spontaneous? Methodical? Creative?
- **How you make decisions:**
  Are you intuitive? Logical? Emotional? Practical? Systematic? Analytical?
- **How you approach life:**
  Are you laid back? Ambitious? Perfectionist? Idealistic? Optimistic? Pessimistic? Self-sufficient?

Feel free to use any of these words if they happen to describe you well, but please don't limit yourself to this list. Pick the best adjectives that paint an accurate picture of the real you. Get more ideas from a dictionary or thesaurus if you'd like.

When you're finished, put the completed list in your Big Question AnswerBook.

Big Activity #1: **who are you?**

fifteen qualities that describe me		
1	2	3
4	5	6
7	8	9
10	11	12
13	14	15
etc.		

Big Question #2: what are your interests and strengths?

For many people, doing something they like to do is the most important part of deciding on a career path—even more important than how much money they can earn!

We don't all like to do the same things—and that's good. For some people, the ideal vacation is lying on a beach, doing absolutely nothing; others would love to spend weeks visiting museums and historic places. Some people wish they had time to learn to skydive or fly a plane; others like to learn to cook gourmet meals or do advanced math.

If we all liked the same things, the world just wouldn't work very well. There would be incredible crowds in some places and ghost towns in others. Some of our natural resources would be overburdened; others would never be used. We would all want to eat at the same restaurant, wear the same outfit, see the same movie, and live in the same place. How boring!

So let's get down to figuring out what you most like to do and how you can spend your working life doing just that. In some ways your answer to this question is all you really need to know about choosing a career, because the people who enjoy their work the most are those who do something they enjoy. We're not talking rocket science here. Just plain old common sense.

Big Activity # 2:

what are your interests and strengths?

Imagine this: No school, no job, no homework, no chores, no obligations at all. All the time in the world you want to do all the things you like most. You know what we're talking about—those things that completely grab your interest and keep you engrossed for hours without your getting bored. Those kinds of things you do really well—sometimes effortlessly, sometimes with extraordinary (and practiced) skill.

And, by the way, EVERYONE has plenty of both interests and strengths. Some are just more visible than others.

Step 1: Write the three things you most enjoy doing on a sheet of paper, if this book doesn't belong to you. Leave lots of space after each thing.

Step 2: Think about some of the deeper reasons why you enjoy each of these activities—the motivations beyond "it's fun." Do you enjoy shopping because it gives you a chance to be with your friends? Because it allows you to find new ways to express your individuality? Because you enjoy the challenge of finding bargains or things no one else has discovered? Or because it's fun to imagine the lifestyle you'll be able to lead when you're finally rich and famous? In the blank spaces, record the reasons why you enjoy each activity.

Step 3: Keep this list handy in your Big Question AnswerBook so that you can refer to it any time you have to make a vocational decision. Sure, you may have to update the list from time to time as your interests change. But one thing is certain. The kind of work you'll most enjoy will be linked in some way to the activities on that list. Count on it.

Maybe one of your favorite things to do is "play basketball." Does that mean the only way you'll ever be happy at work is to play professional basketball?

Maybe.

Maybe not.

Use your *why* responses to read between the lines. The *whys* can prove even more important than the *whats*. Perhaps what you like most about playing basketball is the challenge or the chance to be part of a team that shares a common goal. Maybe you really like pushing yourself to improve. Or it could be the rush associated with competition and the thrill of winning.

The more you uncover your own *whys*, the closer you'll be to discovering important clues about the kinds of work that are best for you.

Big Activity #2: **what are your interests and strengths?**

things you enjoy doing	why you enjoy doing them
1	• • •
2	• • •
3	• • •

Big Question #3: what are your work values?

Chances are, you've never given a moment's thought to this next question. At least not in the context of career planning.

You already looked at who you are and what you enjoy and do well. The idea being, of course, to seek out career options that make the most of your innate qualities, preferences, and natural abilities.

As you start checking into various careers, you'll discover one more dimension associated with making personally appropriate career choices. You'll find that even though people may have the exact same job title, they may execute their jobs in dramatically different ways. For instance, everyone knows about teachers. They teach things to other people. Period.

But wait. If you line up 10 aspiring teachers in one room, you may be surprised to discover how vastly different their interpretations of the job may be. There are the obvious differences, of course. One may want to teach young children; one may want to teach adults. One will focus on teaching math, while another one focuses on teaching Spanish.

Look a little closer and you'll find even greater disparity in the choices they make. One may opt for the prestige (and paycheck) of working in an Ivy League college, while another is completely committed to teaching disadvantaged children in a remote area of the Appalachian Mountains. One may approach teaching simply as a way to make a living, while another devotes almost every waking hour to working with his or her students.

These subtle but significant differences reflect what's truly important to each person. In a word, they reflect the person's values—those things that are most important to them.

People's values depend on many factors—their upbringing, their life experiences, their goals and ambitions, their religious beliefs, and, quite frankly, the way they view the world and their role in it. Very few people share exactly the same values. However, that doesn't necessarily mean that some people are right and others are wrong. It just means they have different perspectives.

Here's a story that shows how different values can be reflected in career choices.

Imagine: It's five years after college graduation and a group of college friends are back together for the first time. They catch up about their lives, their families, and their careers. Listen in on one of their reunion conversations and see if you can guess what each is doing now.

Alice: I have the best career. Every day I get the chance to help kids with special needs get a good education.

Bob: I love my career, too. It's great to know that I am making my town a safer place for everyone.

Cathy: It was tough for me to commit to more school after college. But I'm glad I did. After all I went through when my parents divorced, I'm glad I can be there to make things easier for other families.

David: I know how you feel. I'm glad I get to do something that helps companies function smoothly and keep our economy strong. Of course, you remember that I had a hard time deciding whether to pursue this career or teaching! This way I get the best of both worlds.

Elizabeth: It's great that we both ended up in the corporate world. You know that I was always intrigued by the stock market.

So exactly what is each of the five former freshman friends doing today? Have you made your guesses?

Alice is a lawyer. She specializes in education law. She makes sure that school districts provide special needs children with all of the resources they are entitled to under the law.

Bob is a lawyer. He is a prosecuting attorney and makes his town safer by ensuring that justice is served when someone commits a crime.

Cathy is a lawyer. She practices family law. She helps families negotiate separation and divorce agreements and makes sure that adoption and custody proceedings protect everyone involved. Sometimes she even provides legal intervention to protect adults or children who are in abusive situations.

David is a lawyer. He practices employment law. He helps companies set up policies that follow fair employment practices. He also gives seminars to managers, teaching them what the law says and means about sexual harassment, discrimination, and termination of employment.

Elizabeth is a lawyer. She practices corporate law and is indispensable to corporations with legal responsibilities towards stockholders and the government.

Wow! All five friends have the same job title. But each describes his/her job so differently! All five were able to enter the field of law and focus on the things that are most important to them: quality education, freedom from crime, protection of families and children, fairness in the workplace, and corporate economic growth. Identifying and honoring your personal values is an important part of choosing your life's work.

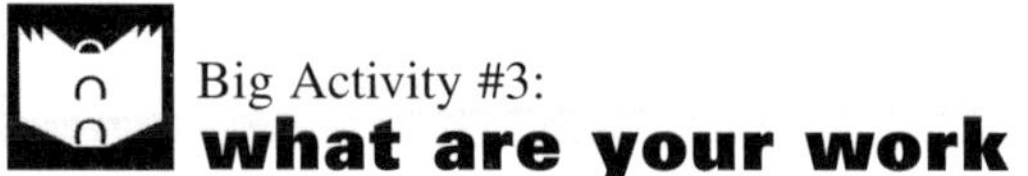

Big Activity #3: **what are your work values?**

Step 1: Look at the following chart. If this book doesn't belong to you, divide a sheet of paper into the following three columns:

- **Essential**

  Statements that fall into this column are very important to you. If the job doesn't satisfy these needs, you're not interested.
- **Okay**

  Great if the job satisfies these needs, but you can also live without them.
- **No Way**

  Statements that fall into this column represent needs that are not at all important to you or things you'd rather do without or simply couldn't tolerate.

Step 2: Look over the following list of statements representing different work values. Rewrite each statement in the appropriate column. Does the first statement represent something that is critical to you to have in your work? If so, write it in the first column. No big deal either way? Write it in the second column. Couldn't stand it? Write it in the third column. Repeat the same process for each of the value statements.

Step 3: When you're finished, place your complete work values chart in your Big Question AnswerBook.

Got it? Then get with it.

Really think about these issues. Lay it on the line. What values are so deeply ingrained in you that you'd be absolutely miserable if you had to sacrifice them for a job? Religious beliefs and political leanings fall into this category for some people.

Which ones provide room for some give and take? Things like vacation and benefits, working hours, and other issues along those lines may be completely negotiable for some people, but absolutely not for others.

Just remember, wherever you go and whatever you do, be sure that the choices you make are true to you.

Big Activity #3: **what are your work values?**

work values	essential	okay	no way
1. I can count on plenty of opportunity for advancement and taking on more responsibility.			
2. I can work to my fullest potential using all of my abilities.			
3. I would be able to give directions and instructions to others.			
4. I would always know exactly what my manager expects of me.			
5. I could structure my own day.			
6. I would be very busy all day.			
7. I would work in attractive and pleasant surroundings.			
8. My coworkers would be people I might choose as friends.			
9. I would get frequent feedback about my performance.			
10. I could continue my education to progress to an even higher level job.			
11. Most of the time I would be able to work alone.			
12. I would know precisely what I need to do to succeed at the job.			
13. I could make decisions on my own.			

Big Activity #3: **what are your work values?**

work values	essential	okay	no way
14. I would have more than the usual amount of vacation time.			
15. I would be working doing something I really believe in.			
16. I would feel like part of a team.			
17. I would find good job security and stable employment opportunities in the industry.			
18. I could depend on my manager for the training I need.			
19. I would earn lots of money.			
20. I would feel a sense of accomplishment in my work.			
21. I would be helping other people.			
22. I could try out my own ideas.			
23. I would not need to have further training or education to do this job.			
24. I would get to travel a lot.			
25. I could work the kind of hours I need to balance work, family, and personal responsibilities.	ESSENTIAL	OKAY	NO WAY

To summarize in my own words, the work values most important to me include:

? Big Question #4: what is your work personality?

Congratulations. After completing the first three activities, you've already discovered a set of skills you can use throughout your life. Basing key career decisions on factors associated with who you are, what you enjoy and do well, and what's most important about work will help you today as you're just beginning to explore the possibilities, as well as into the future as you look for ways to cultivate your career.

Now that you've got that mastered, let's move on to another important skill. This one blends some of what you just learned about yourself with what you need to learn about the real world of work. It's a reality check of sorts as you align and merge your personal interests and abilities with those required in different work situations. At the end of this task you will identify your personal interest profile.

This activity is based on the work of Dr. John Holland. Dr. Holland conducted groundbreaking research that identified different characteristics in people. He found that he could classify people into six basic groups based on which characteristics tended to occur at the same time. He also found that the characteristics that defined the different groups of people were also characteristics that corresponded to success in different groups of occupations. The result of all that work was a classification system that identifies and names six distinct groups of people who share personal interests or characteristics and are likely to be successful in a group of clearly identified jobs.

Dr. Holland's work is respected by workforce professionals everywhere and is widely used by employers and employment agencies to help people get a handle on the best types of work to pursue.

The following Work Interest Profiler (WIP) is based on Dr. Holland's theories and was developed by the U.S. Department of Labor's Employment and Training Administration as part of an important project called O*Net. O*Net is a system used in all 50 states to provide career and employment services to thousands of people every year. It's a system you'll want to know about when it's time to take that first plunge into the world of work. If you'd like, you can find more information about this system at ***http://online.onetcenter.org***.

Big Activity #4:
what is your work personality?

By completing O*Net's Work Interest Profiler (WIP), you'll gain valuable insight into the types of work that are right for you.

here's how it works

The WIP lists many activities that real people do at real jobs. Your task is to read a brief statement about each of these activities and decide if it is something you think you'd enjoy doing. Piece of cake!

Don't worry about whether you have enough education or training to perform the activity. And, for now, forget about how much money you would make performing the activity.

Just boil it down to whether or not you'd like performing each work activity. If you'd like it, put a check in the *like* column that corresponds to each of the six interest areas featured in the test on the handy dandy chart you're about to create (or use the one in the book if it's yours). If you don't like it, put that check in the *dislike* column. What if you don't have a strong opinion on a particular activity? That's okay. Count that one as *unsure*.

Be completely honest with yourself. No one else is going to see your chart. If you check things you think you "should" check, you are not helping yourself find the career that will make you happy.

Before you start, create a chart for yourself. Your scoring sheet will have six horizontal rows and three vertical columns. Label the six rows as Sections 1 through 6, and label the three columns *like*, *dislike*, and *unsure*.

how to complete the Work Interest Profiler

Step 1: Start with Section 1.

Step 2: Look at the first activity and decide whether you would like to do it as part of your job.

Step 3: Put a mark in the appropriate column (*Like*, *Dislike*, or *Unsure*) on the Section 1 row.

Step 4: Continue for every activity in Section 1. Then do Sections 2 through 6.

Step 5: When you've finished all of the sections, count the number of marks you have in each column and write down the total.

Remember, this is not a test! There are no right or wrong answers. You are completing this profile to learn more about yourself and your work-related interests.

Also, once you've completed this activity, be sure to put your chart and any notes in your Big Question AnswerBook.

Ready? Let's go!

Section 1

1. Drive a taxi
2. Repair household appliances
3. Catch fish as a member of a fishing crew
4. Paint houses
5. Assemble products in a factory
6. Install flooring in houses
7. Perform lawn care services
8. Drive a truck to deliver packages to homes and offices
9. Work on an offshore oil-drilling rig
10. Put out forest fires
11. Fix a broken faucet
12. Refinish furniture
13. Guard money in an armored car
14. Lay brick or tile
15. Operate a dairy farm
16. Raise fish in a fish hatchery
17. Build a brick walkway
18. Enforce fish and game laws
19. Assemble electronic parts
20. Build kitchen cabinets
21. Maintain the grounds of a park
22. Operate a motorboat to carry passengers
23. Set up and operate machines to make products
24. Spray trees to prevent the spread of harmful insects
25. Monitor a machine on an assembly line

Section 2

1. Study space travel
2. Develop a new medicine
3. Study the history of past civilizations
4. Develop a way to better predict the weather
5. Determine the infection rate of a new disease
6. Study the personalities of world leaders
7. Investigate the cause of a fire
8. Develop psychological profiles of criminals
9. Study whales and other types of marine life
10. Examine blood samples using a microscope
11. Invent a replacement for sugar
12. Study genetics
13. Do research on plants or animals
14. Study weather conditions
15. Investigate crimes
16. Study ways to reduce water pollution
17. Develop a new medical treatment or procedure
18. Diagnose and treat sick animals
19. Conduct chemical experiments
20. Study rocks and minerals
21. Do laboratory tests to identify diseases
22. Study the structure of the human body
23. Plan a research study
24. Study the population growth of a city
25. Make a map of the bottom of the ocean

Section 3

1. Paint sets for a play
2. Create special effects for movies
3. Write reviews of books or movies
4. Compose or arrange music
5. Design artwork for magazines
6. Pose for a photographer
7. Create dance routines for a show
8. Play a musical instrument
9. Edit movies
10. Sing professionally
11. Announce a radio show
12. Perform stunts for a movie or television show
13. Design sets for plays
14. Act in a play
15. Write a song
16. Perform jazz or tap dance
17. Sing in a band
18. Direct a movie
19. Write scripts for movies or television shows
20. Audition singers and musicians for a musical show
21. Conduct a musical choir
22. Perform comedy routines in front of an audience
23. Dance in a Broadway show
24. Perform as an extra in movies, plays, or television shows
25. Write books or plays

Section 4

1. Teach children how to play sports
2. Help people with family-related problems
3. Teach an individual an exercise routine
4. Perform nursing duties in a hospital
5. Help people with personal or emotional problems
6. Teach work and living skills to people with disabilities
7. Assist doctors in treating patients
8. Work with juveniles on probation
9. Supervise the activities of children at a camp
10. Teach an elementary school class
11. Perform rehabilitation therapy
12. Help elderly people with their daily activities
13. Help people who have problems with drugs or alcohol
14. Teach a high school class
15. Give career guidance to people
16. Do volunteer work at a non-profit organization
17. Help families care for ill relatives
18. Teach sign language to people with hearing disabilities
19. Help people with disabilities improve their daily living skills
20. Help conduct a group therapy session
21. Work with children with mental disabilities
22. Give CPR to someone who has stopped breathing
23. Provide massage therapy to people
24. Plan exercises for patients with disabilities
25. Counsel people who have a life-threatening illness

Section 5

1. Sell CDs and tapes at a music store
2. Manage a clothing store
3. Sell houses
4. Sell computer equipment in a store
5. Operate a beauty salon or barber shop
6. Sell automobiles
7. Represent a client in a lawsuit
8. Negotiate business contracts
9. Sell a soft drink product line to stores and restaurants
10. Start your own business
11. Be responsible for the operations of a company
12. Give a presentation about a product you are selling
13. Buy and sell land
14. Sell restaurant franchises to individuals
15. Manage the operations of a hotel
16. Negotiate contracts for professional athletes
17. Sell merchandise at a department store
18. Market a new line of clothing
19. Buy and sell stocks and bonds
20. Sell merchandise over the telephone
21. Run a toy store
22. Sell hair-care products to stores and salons
23. Sell refreshments at a movie theater
24. Manage a retail store
25. Sell telephone and other communication equipment

Section 6

1. Develop an office filing system
2. Generate the monthly payroll checks for an office
3. Proofread records or forms
4. Schedule business conferences
5. Enter information into a database
6. Photocopy letters and reports
7. Keep inventory records
8. Record information from customers applying for charge accounts
9. Load computer software into a large computer network
10. Use a computer program to generate customer bills
11. Develop a spreadsheet using computer software
12. Operate a calculator
13. Direct or transfer office phone calls
14. Use a word processor to edit and format documents
15. Transfer funds between banks, using a computer
16. Compute and record statistical and other numerical data
17. Stamp, sort, and distribute office mail
18. Maintain employee records
19. Record rent payments
20. Keep shipping and receiving records
21. Keep accounts payable/receivable for an office
22. Type labels for envelopes and packages
23. Calculate the wages of employees
24. Take notes during a meeting
25. Keep financial records

Section 1
Realistic

	Like	Dislike	Unsure
1.			
2.			
3.			
4.			
5.			
6.			
7.			
8.			
9.			
10.			
11.			
12.			
13.			
14.			
15.			
16.			
17.			
18.			
19.			
20.			
21.			
22.			
23.			
24.			
25.			

Total Realistic

Section 2
Investigative

	Like	Dislike	Unsure
1.			
2.			
3.			
4.			
5.			
6.			
7.			
8.			
9.			
10.			
11.			
12.			
13.			
14.			
15.			
16.			
17.			
18.			
19.			
20.			
21.			
22.			
23.			
24.			
25.			

Total Investigative

Section 3
Artistic

	Like	Dislike	Unsure
1.			
2.			
3.			
4.			
5.			
6.			
7.			
8.			
9.			
10.			
11.			
12.			
13.			
14.			
15.			
16.			
17.			
18.			
19.			
20.			
21.			
22.			
23.			
24.			
25.			

Total Artistic

Section 4
Social

	Like	Dislike	Unsure
1.			
2.			
3.			
4.			
5.			
6.			
7.			
8.			
9.			
10.			
11.			
12.			
13.			
14.			
15.			
16.			
17.			
18.			
19.			
20.			
21.			
22.			
23.			
24.			
25.			

Total Social

Section 5
Enterprising

	Like	Dislike	Unsure
1.			
2.			
3.			
4.			
5.			
6.			
7.			
8.			
9.			
10.			
11.			
12.			
13.			
14.			
15.			
16.			
17.			
18.			
19.			
20.			
21.			
22.			
23.			
24.			
25.			

Total Enterprising

Section 6
Conventional

	Like	Dislike	Unsure
1.			
2.			
3.			
4.			
5.			
6.			
7.			
8.			
9.			
10.			
11.			
12.			
13.			
14.			
15.			
16.			
17.			
18.			
19.			
20.			
21.			
22.			
23.			
24.			
25.			

Total Conventional

What are your top three work personalities? List them here if this is your own book or on a separate piece of paper if it's not.

1. ______
2. ______
3. ______

all done? let's see what it means

Be sure you count up the number of marks in each column on your scoring sheet and write down the total for each column. You will probably notice that you have a lot of *like*s for some sections, and a lot of *dislike*s for other sections. The section that has the most *like*s is your primary interest area. The section with the next highest number of *like*s is your second interest area. The next highest is your third interest area.

Now that you know your top three interest areas, what does it mean about your work personality type? We'll get to that in a minute, but first we are going to answer a couple of other questions that might have crossed your mind:

- What is the best work personality to have?
- What does my work personality mean?

First of all, there is no "best" personality in general. There is, however, a "best" personality for each of us. It's who we really are and how we feel most comfortable. There may be several "best" work personalities for any job because different people may approach the job in different ways. But there is no "best work personality."

Asking about the "best work personality" is like asking whether the "best" vehicle is a sports car, a sedan, a station wagon, or a sports utility vehicle. It all depends on who you are and what you need.

One thing we do know is that our society needs all of the work personalities in order to function effectively. Fortunately, we usually seem to have a good mix of each type.

So, while many people may find science totally boring, there are many other people who find it fun and exciting. Those are the people who invent new technologies, who become doctors and researchers, and who turn natural resources into the things we use every day. Many people may think that spending a day with young children is unbearable, but those who love that environment are the teachers, community leaders, and museum workers that nurture children's minds and personalities.

When everything is in balance, there's a job for every person and a person for every job.

Now we'll get to your work personality. Following are descriptions of each of Dr. Holland's six work personalities that correspond to the six sections in your last exercise. You, like most people, are a unique combination of more than one. A little of this, a lot of that. That's what makes us interesting.

Identify your top three work personalities. Also, pull out your responses to the first three exercises we did. As you read about your top three work personalities, see how they are similar to the way you described yourself earlier.

Type 1
Realistic

Realistic people are often seen as the "Doers." They have mechanical or athletic ability and enjoy working outdoors.

Realistic people like work activities that include practical, hands-on problems and solutions. They enjoy dealing with plants, animals, and real-life materials like wood, tools, and machinery.

Careers that involve a lot of paperwork or working closely with others are usually not attractive to realistic people.

Who you are:
independent
reserved
practical
mechanical
athletic
persistent

What you like to do/what you do well:
build things
train animals
play a sport
fix things
garden
hunt or fish
woodworking
repair cars
refinish furniture

Career possibilities:
aerospace engineer
aircraft pilot
animal breeder
architect
baker/chef
building inspector
carpenter
chemical engineer
civil engineer
construction manager
dental assistant
detective
glazier
jeweler
machinist
oceanographer
optician
park ranger
plumber
police officer
practical nurse
private investigator
radiologist
sculptor

Type 2
Investigative

Investigative people are often seen as the "Thinkers." They much prefer searching for facts and figuring out problems mentally to doing physical activity or leading other people.

If Investigative is one of your strong interest areas, your answers to the earlier exercises probably matched some of these:

Who you are:
curious
logical
independent
analytical
observant
inquisitive

What you like to do/what you do well:
think abstractly
solve problems
use a microscope
do research
fly a plane
explore new subjects
study astronomy
do puzzles
work with a computer

Career possibilities:

aerospace engineer
archaeologist
CAD technician
chemist
chiropractor
computer programmer
coroner
dentist
electrician
ecologist
geneticist
hazardous waste technician
historian
horticulturist
management consultant
medical technologist
meteorologist
nurse practitioner
pediatrician
pharmacist
political scientist
psychologist
software engineer
surgeon
technical writer
veterinarian
zoologist

Type 3
Artistic

Artistic people are the "Creators." People with this primary interest like work activities that deal with the artistic side of things.

Artistic people need to have the opportunity for self-expression in their work. They want to be able to use their imaginations and prefer to work in less structured environments, without clear sets of rules about how things should be done.

Who you are:

imaginative
intuitive
expressive
emotional
creative
independent

What you like to do/what you do well:

draw
paint
play an instrument
visit museums
act
design clothes or rooms
read fiction
travel
write stories, poetry, or music

Career possibilities:

architect
actor
animator
art director
cartoonist
choreographer
costume designer
composer
copywriter
dancer
disc jockey
drama teacher
emcee
fashion designer
graphic designer
illustrator
interior designer
journalist
landscape architect
medical illustrator
photographer
producer
scriptwriter
set designer

Type 4
Social

Social people are known as the "Helpers." They are interested in work that can assist others and promote learning and personal development.

Communication with other people is very important to those in the Social group. They usually do not enjoy jobs that require a great amount of work with objects, machines, or data. Social people like to teach, give advice, help, cure, or otherwise be of service to people.

Who you are:
friendly
outgoing
empathic
persuasive
idealistic
generous

What you like to do/what you do well:
teach others
work in groups
play team sports
care for children
go to parties
help or advise others
meet new people
express yourself
join clubs or organizations

Career possibilities:
animal trainer
arbitrator
art teacher
art therapist
audiologist
child care worker
clergy person
coach
counselor/therapist
cruise director
dental hygienist
employment interviewer
EMT worker
fitness trainer
flight attendant
occupational therapist
police officer
recreational therapist
registered nurse
school psychologist
social worker
substance abuse counselor
teacher
tour guide

Type 5
Enterprising

Enterprising work personalities can be called the "Persuaders." These people like work activities that have to do with starting up and carrying out projects, especially business ventures. They like taking risks for profit, enjoy being responsible for making decisions, and generally prefer action to thought or analysis.

People in the Enterprising group like to work with other people. While the Social group focuses on helping other people, members of the Enterprising group are able to lead, manage, or persuade other people to accomplish the goals of the organization.

Who you are:
assertive
self-confident
ambitious
extroverted
optimistic
adventurous

What you like to do/what you do well:
organize activities
sell things
promote ideas

discuss politics
hold office in clubs
give talks or speeches
meet people
initiate projects
start your own business

Career possibilities:
advertising
chef
coach, scout
criminal investigator
economist
editor
foreign service officer
funeral director
hotel manager
journalist
lawyer
lobbyist
public relations specialist
newscaster
restaurant manager
sales manager
school principal
ship's captain
stockbroker
umpire, referee
urban planner

Type 6 Conventional

People in the Conventional group are the "Organizers." They like work activities that follow set procedures and routines. They are more comfortable and proficient working with data and detail than they are with generalized ideas.

Conventional people are happiest in work situations where the lines of authority are clear, where they know exactly what responsibilities are expected of them, and where there are precise standards for the work.

Who you are:
well-organized
accurate
practical
persistent
conscientious
ambitious

What you like to do/what you do well:
work with numbers
type accurately
collect or organize things
follow up on tasks
be punctual
be responsible for details
proofread
keep accurate records
understand regulations

Career possibilities:
accountant
actuary
air traffic controller
assessor
budget analyst
building inspector
chief financial officer
corporate treasurer
cost estimator
court reporter
economist
environmental compliance lawyer
fire inspector
insurance underwriter
legal secretary
mathematician
medical secretary
proofreader
tax preparer

arts and communications careers work personality chart

Once you've discovered your own unique work personality code, you can use it to explore the careers profiled in this book and elsewhere. Do keep in mind though that this code is just a tool meant to help focus your search. It's not meant to box you in or to keep you from pursuing any career that happens to capture your imagination.

Following is a chart listing the work personality codes associated with each of the careers profiled in this book.

	Realistic	Investigative	Artistic	Social	Enterprising	Conventional
My Work Personality Code (mark your top three areas)						
Actor			X	X	X	
Animator			X	X	X	
Art Director			X	X	X	
Art Therapist			X	X	X	
Arts Administrator			X	X	X	
Arts Teacher			X	X	X	
Broadcast Technician	X				X	X
CAD (Computer-Aided Design) Technician	X	X			X	
Choreographer			X	X	X	
Cinematographer			X	X	X	
Commercial Artist			X	X	X	
Corporate Communications Director				X	X	X
Costume Designer	X		X	X		
Dancer	X		X		X	
Development Director			X	X	X	
Editor			X	X	X	
Fashion Designer	X		X	X		

	Realistic	Investigative	Artistic	Social	Enterprising	Conventional
My Work Personality Code (mark your top three areas)						
Film Director	X			X		X
Graphic Designer	X		X		X	
Illustrator	X		X		X	
Interior Designer	X		X		X	
Journalist		X	X		X	
Lighting Technician	X	X	X			
Lobbyist			X	X	X	
Museum Curator	X	X		X		
Music Composer			X	X	X	
Musician			X	X		X
Photographer	X		X	X		
Printer	X	X			X	
Public Relations Specialist			X	X	X	
Publisher		X		X	X	
Scriptwriter		X	X		X	
Set and Exhibit Designer		X	X	X		
Technical Writer	X	X		X		
Webmaster		X			X	X
Writer		X	X		X	

Now it's time to move on to the next big step in the Big Question process. While the first step focused on you, the next one focuses on the world of work. It includes profiles of a wide variety of occupations related to the arts and communications, a roundtable discussion with professionals working in these fields, and a mind-boggling list of other careers to consider when wanting to blend passion or talent in these areas with your life's work.

SECTION 2 explore your options

By now you probably have a fairly good understanding of the assets (some fully realized and perhaps others only partially developed) that you bring to your future career. You've defined key characteristics about yourself, identified special interests and strengths, examined your work values, and analyzed your basic work personality traits. All in all, you've taken a good, hard look at yourself and we're hoping that you're encouraged by all the potential you've discovered.

Now it's time to look at the world of work.

In the following section, you'll find in-depth profiles of 36 careers representing the arts, communications, and entertainment industry. Some of these careers you may already know about. Others will present new ideas for your consideration. All are part of a dynamic and important segment of the U.S. economy.

When exploring careers in the arts and communications, it may help to know that we've included six basic directions or "pathways" to consider. Understanding these pathways provides another important clue about which direction might be best for you. The six arts and communications pathways include

Audiovisual Communications Technology

According to experts associated with the U.S. Department of Education's Career Cluster initiative, people who work in audiovisual (AV) commu-

fyi Each of the following profiles includes several common elements to help guide you through an effective career exploration process. For each career, you'll find

- A sidebar loaded with information you can use to find out more about the profession. Professional associations, pertinent reading materials, the lowdown on wages and suggested training requirements, and a list of typical types of employers are all included to give you a broader view of what the career is all about.
- An informative essay describing what the career involves.
- Get Started Now strategies you can use right now to get prepared, test the waters, and develop your skills.
- A Hire Yourself project providing realistic activities like those you would actually find on the job. Try these learning activities and find out what it's really like to be a . . . you name it.

You don't have to read the profiles in order. You may want to first browse through the career ideas that appear to be most interesting. Then check out the others—you never know what might interest you when you know more about it. As you read each profile, think about how well it matches up with what you learned about yourself in Section 1: **Discover You at Work**. Narrow down your options to a few careers and use the rating system described below to evaluate your interest levels.

- **No way!** There's not even a remote chance that this career is a good fit for me. (Since half of figuring out what you do want to do in life involves figuring out what you don't want to do, this is not a bad place to be.)
- **This is intriguing.** I want to learn more about it and look at similar careers as well. (The activities outlined in Section 3: **Experiment with Success** will be especially useful in this regard.)
- **This is it!** It's the career I've been looking for all my life and I want to go after it with all I've got. (Head straight to Section 3: **Experiment with Success**.)

nications generally manufacture, sell, rent, design, operate, and repair the equipment used in audiovisual communications. They use sophisticated equipment to present sound, video, and data to a wide variety of audiences in corporate boardrooms, hotels, convention centers, classrooms, theme parks, stadiums, and museums. AV careers profiled in this book include broadcast technician and lighting technician.

Broadcast, Film, and Journalism

Professionals involved in broadcast, film, and journalism are the people who inform the world about local, state, national, and international events by preparing stories and information for newspapers, books, and magazines; radio, television, and Internet broadcasts; and presenting various points of view on current events in a wide range of multimedia formats. Broadcast, film, and journalism careers profiled in this book include editor, journalist, publisher, technical writer, webmaster, and writer.

Performing Arts

This segment of the industry includes both the performers who appear onstage and onscreen in televised, theatrical, and musical productions and all the many professionals who work behind the scenes to make possible these productions. Performing arts professions featured in this book include actor, animator, arts administrator, arts teacher, choreographer, cinematographer, costume designer, dancer, film director, museum curator, music composer, musician, scriptwriter, and set and exhibit designer.

Printing Technology

Professionals in printing technology work in one of three stages involved in the printing process—prepress, press, and binding (or postpress). Together, their job is to transform text and pictures (and, increasingly, digital files) into finished pages used in publications such as books, magazines, newspapers, brochures, and posters. Printing Technology professions covered in this book include graphic designer and printer.

Public Relations and Business Communications

Public relations and business communications cover a wide variety of professions related to creating public awareness for and representing the interests of private and public organizations such as corporations and government. Public relations and business communications careers profiled in this book include art director, corporate communications director, development director, lobbyist, and public relations specialist.

A Note on Websites

Websites tend to move around a bit. If you have trouble finding a particular site, use an Internet browser to search for a specific website or type of information.

Visual Arts

The visual arts represent all the professionals who create art to communicate ideas, thoughts, and feelings using any of a number of media such as painting, photography, and illustration. Visual artists are generally classified into two groups: fine artists, whose art is a means of self-expression; and commercial artists, whose artistic talents are applied to serve the specific needs of clients or corporations. Visual arts professions included in this book include CAD (computer-aided design) technician, commercial artist, fashion designer, illustrator, interior designer, and photographer.

As you explore the individual careers in this book and others in this series, remember to keep what you've learned about yourself in mind. Consider each option in light of what you know about your interests, strengths, work values, and work personality.

Pay close attention to the job requirements. Does it require math aptitude? Good writing skills? Ability to take things apart and visualize how they go back together? If you don't have the necessary abilities (and don't have a strong desire to acquire them), you probably won't enjoy the job.

For instance, several popular TV shows make forensic investigation look like a fascinating career. And it is—for some people. But when considering whether forensic investigation—or any career for that matter—is right for you, think about the skills it takes to succeed. In this case, we're talking about lots of chemistry, anatomy, and physics. And, quite frankly, working with dead people. Be realistic about each profession so that you can make an honest assessment of how appropriate it is for you.

actor They make you laugh. They make you cry. They make you think. At least, that's what happens when actors do the job right. If you think acting is simply a matter of reading lines from a script, you've got it all wrong. In order to keep the applause (and the paychecks!) coming, actors have to assume completely new personas. Through words, actions, and emotions, they draw audiences into stories that entertain, educate, or enlighten. Whether on stage at a community theater or appearing in full living color on television or in a movie, actors become the ultimate communicators.

Competition is fierce in this industry. There are a lot of talented people out there hoping to be the next Tom Hanks or Julia Roberts. Entertainment magazines are full of stories about famous actors talking about their "lucky breaks." A little reading between the lines, however, often reveals that these "breaks" came after years of hard work and disappointment. According to well-known actor Charles Grodin, an actor doesn't need one lucky break; he or she needs 100. To land a good part in a play, movie, television show, or commercial, actors (even famous ones) typically audition, often competing for roles with hundreds of other applicants. Successful actors need patience and commitment since they can go through long stretches of waiting—often needing to work other jobs—before they land a role.

Does that mean that aspiring actors should give up their dreams?

Get Started Now!

Raise the curtain on your acting career by using these strategies:

- Get involved in a school or local theater production.
- Enroll in any classes that get you talking—drama, speech, debate, etc.
- Work to perfect your performance résumé by studying dance and music.

Search It!
The Screen Actors Guild (SAG) at ***www.sag.org/wannabe.html***

Read It!
Backstage newspaper at ***www.backstage.com***

Learn It!
- Bachelor's degree in theater, theater arts, or performing arts is encouraged but not required
- Experience in local and regional theater productions

Earn It!
Median annual salary is $26,460. (Source: U.S. Department of Labor)

Find It!
Actors find work through on-line casting calls such as ***www.showbiz.com/castingcalls.php*** and ***www.auditionfirm.com***; Hollywood studios such as ***www.dreamworks.com***; entertainment venues such as ***http://disney.go.com/disneycareers***; and talent agencies such as the William Morris Agency ***www.wma.com***.

Hire Yourself!

Your agent just called. You've been invited to audition for the lead role in an updated remake of William Shakespeare's timeless classic, *Romeo and Juliet*. According to the casting director's instructions, you need to prepare an original reading based on a favorite scene. That means you have to stay true to the original play while adding your own contemporary interpretation.

To prepare yourself for the role, read the Bard's actual words at ***http://the-tech.mit.edu/Shakespeare/romeo_juliet***. Then compare it with the more contemporary movie version starring Leonardo DiCaprio and Claire Danes (check with your local video store to rent a copy of this 1996 version of *Romeo and Juliet*).

Absolutely not. It means that they should come into the profession with a realistic sense of what it takes and some creative ideas of how to use their talent in ways that may or may not result in an Oscar nomination. Oh, and don't forget the day job. A good back-up job comes in handy when acting gigs are scarce.

That said, there is some good news for aspiring actors. With increasing numbers of cable television channels producing their own programming, more emphasis on using multimedia to create educational videos and Internet content, and a surge in the numbers of community theaters and drama studios, there are more venues than ever before to pursue nontraditional acting careers.

Also, keep in mind that acting isn't the only exciting profession associated with the entertainment business. A look behind the scenes of Broadway shows like *The Producers* or *The Lion King* or a peek at the credits at the end of a movie prove that actors don't succeed on their own. It takes teamwork to create a hit. This team includes directors, lighting crew, sound people, makeup specialists, special effects experts, and an amazing number of other professionals.

Of course, cities like Los Angeles, New York, or Chicago will continue to buzz with film production, television studios, and live theater. If you've got the acting bug—and the talent and guts it takes to ride it out—the show must go on!

animator

animator The ultimate dream job of doodlers everywhere! Creative flair is certainly a big part of the job, but top-notch animators are at least as computer savvy as they are artistic. This blend of artistic talent and technical expertise constitutes the basic prerequisite for creating images that mimic spontaneous lifelike movement for use in movies, television, computer games, and other Web applications. Which is a fancy way of saying that animators use computers to create "eye candy" for an ever-growing array of media outlets.

Animation is no longer just for kiddie cartoons. Homer Simpson has seen to that. Kids and adults alike enjoy the "sky is the limit" aspect of what animation studios are producing these days. In fact, audiences for animated features have grown so attractive that Disney, Warner Brothers, 20th Century Fox, Viacom, and DreamWorks are all spending big bucks to expand their respective animation departments.

Other skills that come into play involve—surprise!—science and math. Anatomy, physics, geometry—they all merge together when depicting people, places, and things in action.

Good animators make the job look easy, but in reality, it's a complicated process involving four key steps. First comes the idea—that amazing place where all things creative begin. Then come storyboards—the essential process of explaining the idea and illustrating the sequence of action as the story unfolds. When finished, storyboards look a lot like comic strip panels. Next comes the technical part. This step is called

Get Started Now!

Use these strategies to get ready for a future in animation:

- Take as many art, drawing, and computer graphics classes as you can.
- Watch animated movies and cartoon shows both old and new.
- Check out good college and art school programs.

Search It!
SIGGRAPH (Special Interest Group on Computer Graphics and Interactive Techniques) at ***www.siggraph.org***

Read It!
Animation Magazine at ***www.animationmagazine.net*** and "Making Digits Dance: Visual Effects and Animation Careers in the Entertainment Industry" at ***www.eidc.com/MDD.pdf***

Learn It!

- Four-year college degree in art, film, or graphic design
- Two-year art school degree in animation, multimedia design, or graphic design

Earn It!
Median annual salary is $45,920. (Source: U.S. Department of Labor)

Find It!
Big name employers in animation include Disney at ***www.disney.com***, LucasArts at ***www.lucasarts.com***, Pixar at ***www.pixar.com***, and Warner Brothers at ***www2.warnerbros.com***.

Hire Yourself

Your client is a television production company. The company is preparing a documentary about what it's like to be a teen in America—the good side and the bad. They want you to develop a five-minute animated clip about fun and trendy aspects of contemporary teen life.

Your job is to create storyboards (at least six panels) that accurately communicate your ideas to the client.

"modeling" and involves using technology to create the illusion of movement and dimension.

Now, finally, let the animation begin! This could take a while. It's not unusual for an animator to produce 160 to 320 drawings in just one week's time. A movie on the scale of Disney's *Beauty and the Beast* easily includes upwards of 120,000 drawings.

Disney's *Dinosaur* involved 50 animators and over 3 million hours of computer time. When all was said and done, it took 70,000 CD-ROMs to store all the work that became an 82-minute film.

All this work generally takes place in animation studios, graphic design companies, or software development firms. These types of businesses often hire both full-time employees and freelancers. Freelancing, a form of self-employment, is a popular option for experienced animators with good professional contacts.

art director Remember the days of show and tell? Art directors take that process to new limits with a "why say it when you can show it" attitude. Whether the medium of choice is a magazine, newspaper, television commercial, or website, art directors are never content to just say it; they have to show it too. Visual communication is the name of their game.

But, as the "director" part of the job title may imply, art directors don't do the job alone. First and foremost, the art director serves as liaison between the client and the company. Creativity and artistic flair, while key requisites for this job, only go so far if clients don't get the results they want. So the art director talks with clients, listens to clients, works very hard to get inside the minds of clients—all in order to deliver a pitch that meets the needs. Since projects requiring art directors—big ad campaigns, feature films, e-commerce websites, all manner of media publications—tend to have big budgets attached, it stands to reason that clients expect to get as much bang for their bucks as possible.

Once client expectations are understood, art directors really get to work—and get their team members working too. Art directors are typically in charge of the "big picture." Budgets, staff, deadlines, and managing all the nitty-gritty details associated with actually executing the plan make up a big part of the art director's job, as does managing the

Get Started Now!

Visualize yourself as an art director.

- Sign up to work on your school newspaper, student magazine, or yearbook to get a hands-on sense of what it takes to pull a publication together.
- Enroll in graphic design and art appreciation courses at your school.
- Look into graphic design internships at your local newspaper or with publishing firms in your area.

Search It!
The Art Directors Club at ***www.adcny.org***

Read It!
Adweek at ***www.adweek.com***, *Graphic Arts Monthly* at ***www.gammag.com***, *Communication Arts* at ***www.commarts.com***, *Print* magazine at ***www.printmag.com***, and *Advertising Age* at ***www.adage.com***

Learn It!
Two- or four-year degree in art, communication arts, advertising, or design

Earn It!
Median annual salary is $62,260. (Source: U.S. Department of Labor)

Find It!
Check out job opportunities with some of the world's largest media giants: Time Warner at ***www.timewarner.com***, Disney at ***www.disney.go.com***, Bertelsmann at ***www.bertelsmann.com***, and Porter Novelli at ***www.porternovelli.com***.

Hire Yourself!

You're young. You're hip. Your client wants to know what you'd like to see in a new on-line "fanzine" (a website devoted to a specific interest) about teen hobbies. Pick a hobby and create an outline describing the types of information, activities, and graphics you'd like to see. Use color and graphics to sketch out what would appear on each page.

Serious and scholarly? Trendy and fun? Think about your audience—fellow hobbyists in this case—and come up with ideas that would appeal to them.

Depending on your skill and available resources, you may sketch the diagram by hand or use a computer. Just think it through and present your ideas clearly. Pen and pencil outlines are acceptable, but for an extra challenge, try your hand at working on-line. For a free tutorial, check out ***www.web-source.net*** or ***www.boogiejack.com***.

work of team members that, depending on the scope of a given project, might include graphic designers, editors, copywriters, photographers, set designers, production staff, and any number of assistants and support personnel.

Art directors generally work their way up to the top and often start as graphic designers. Besides the requisite design and technology skills, art directors bring experience, and in many cases, an impressive track record of success to the job. Management skills and people skills can be acquired on the job or through advanced training at the college level.

Success is in the details as art directors work from concept to completion. An art director's job is done when a project is delivered on time, within budget, and to the absolute satisfaction of the client.

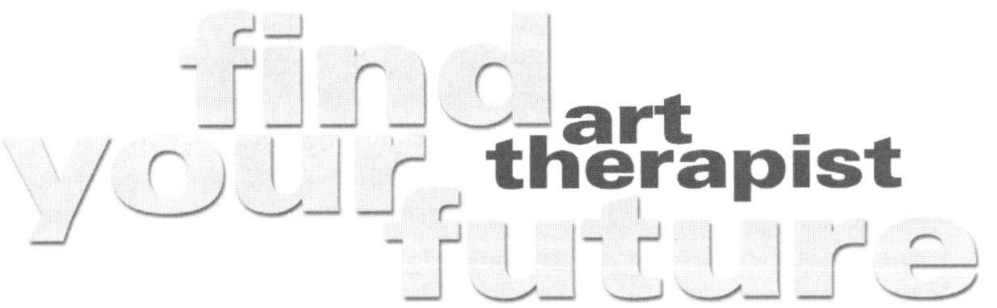

art therapist

Art therapists use art to help people solve problems and recognize potential in their lives. According to the American Art Therapy Association, creating and reflecting on art products and processes helps people "increase awareness of self and others; cope with symptoms, stress, and traumatic experiences; and enhances cognitive abilities."

Art therapists' work proves the credo that a picture is worth a thousand words by providing patients with a way of expressing issues that they may be unable to articulate in words. As the job title implies, art therapists are trained in both art and therapy. They study human development, psychological theories, and spiritual, cultural, and artistic traditions, and they understand the healing power of art.

Art therapy can be an empowering process for many patients. Imagine the difficulties an autistic child must have communicating. Letting that child paint freely on a canvas can open a door of communication. Not only can autistic children express themselves more easily this way, but also it gives them a sense of accomplishment, pride, and joy as they produce their own works of art.

These same principles can help a range of patients, from elderly people who are suffering from depression to those who are undergoing emotional distress from a divorce or death in the family. When some matters are especially hard to talk about, art can be a means of expression that leads to better understanding and coping.

Get Started Now!

Create a career in art therapy:

- Enroll in art courses at school and through any art-related community organizations you can find.
- Be sure to sign up for psychology courses in school.
- Volunteer at health care institutions or rehabilitation centers that have art therapy departments.

Search It!
American Art Therapy Association at ***www.arttherapy.org***

Read It!
Articles at ***www.arttherapy.org/resources/online_articles.htm*** and a career profile at ***www.ama-assn.org/ama/pub/category/10481.html***

Learn It!

- At least a bachelor's degree in counseling or psychology, with a background in art
- The American Art Therapy Association lists approved colleges and universities at ***www.arttherapy.org/ApprovedEducationPrograms.htm***

Earn It!
Average annual salary ranges from $28,000 to $40,000.
(Source: The American Medical Association)

Find It!
Explore job opportunities at ***www.arttherapy.org/members/statechapters.htm*** and ***www.doctorjob.com/careersearch***.

Art therapists meet patients individually or in groups, treating them in meeting rooms, art spaces, or private offices. At first, the job sounds as simple as handing out art supplies and talking about the results. But that's not the case. Art therapists are highly trained professionals who must work from a position of expertise in both the world of art and world of therapy to meet patients' needs. This type of work demands a commitment of several years of intense study. However, it's an investment well worth making for the person interested in using art to help others.

Hire Yourself!

Analyze this! A museum curator wants to mount an exhibit called "Psychology in Painting." He's asked you to choose five paintings that may reveal deep emotional or psychological issues that the artist was grappling with. Go on-line to ***www.artcyclopedia.com*** and browse the virtual art collections of work by many of the world's greatest artists. Pick five examples of work you find particularly interesting. Print out copies and write short paragraphs describing your impressions of the emotional impact of each example.

arts administrator

If it's true that, as the old song goes, there's no business like show business, then it's certainly true that there's no show business without arts administrators. Arts administrators are business managers who take care of behind-the-scenes details that make it possible for art galleries, museums, dance troupes, symphonies, production studios, and even school districts to do what they do so well—entertain, enlighten, and educate.

It probably won't come as much of a surprise to learn that one of the primary job responsibilities of arts administrators involves money—raising it, managing it, and spending it.

A top priority for many arts administrators is making sure that there's at least as much money coming into an organization as there is going out. Budget planning, fund-raising, and strategic planning are all part of the job. Since most arts organizations rely on a variety of sources for income—including everything from ticket sales and corporate sponsorships to government grants and product licensing—this process takes more than a little ingenuity.

Spending the money wisely often becomes an even greater challenge. A theater group with a limited budget, for example, will have to

Get Started Now!

A career in arts administration starts with these steps:

- Indulge your interest in all things artistic by taking relevant courses in school; participating in dance, music, or art programs; and volunteering with local arts groups.
- Work a fund-raiser. See what it really takes to ask people to donate money to a good cause.
- Research colleges that offer programs in arts administration or nonprofit management.

Search It!
National Association of Performing Arts Managers at ***www.napama.org*** and Association of Arts Administration Educators at ***www.artsnet.org/aaae/aaaemain.html***

Read It!
Explore current art happenings at the National Endowment for the Arts website at ***www.arts.endow.gov/explore*** or the Smithsonian's on-line arts ezine at ***www.si.edu/art_and_design/***.

Learn It!
- Bachelor's degree in fine arts, arts administration, nonprofit management, or business administration
- Art-related internships

Earn It!
Entry-level salaries in mid-$20,000s (Source: Carnegie Mellon)

Find It!
Arts organizations include the Alvin Ailey American Dance Theatre at ***www.alvinailey.org***, Chicago Museum of Contemporary Art at ***www.mca.chicago.org***, and the Smithsonian at ***www.si.org***.

Hire Yourself!

It's your lucky day. You are arts administrator for a big metropolitan school district. The Rock and Roll Hall of Fame and Museum (***www.rockhall.com/exhibitions/traveling.asp***) has just announced that it will bring its new traveling exhibition to just 10 school districts this year and your district is at the top of the list.

You think the show offers a great opportunity to provide an unusual and enjoyable art experience for families in your district. The only catch is the price tag—a hefty $100,000 for a three-day run. You've already received a $25,000 grant from the National Endowment for the Arts (***www.nea.gov***), the local arts council has kicked in $15,000, and you expect to earn at least $30,000 in ticket sales. That leaves $30,000.

Your job is to devise a workable plan to come up with the rest of the dough. Your plan might include corporate sponsorships, fundraising events, other grants, or collaboration with other organizations. Get creative, crunch the numbers, and create a PowerPoint presentation that highlights your ideas for the next school board meeting.

carefully apportion how funds are doled out. How much advertising will be purchased on radio, in newspapers, and on TV? How many staff will be hired and how will actors, ticket takers, lighting crew, and other personnel be paid? How much can the group afford to pay in rent?

Beyond financial matters, administrators also have a say in planning annual calendars, hiring staff and talent, making acquisitions (an especially important role in museums and art galleries), and cultivating positive community relations. With responsibility for all these functions, it goes without saying that art administrators need a versatile array of skills. Strong verbal and written communication skills are a must, as is a good grasp of key business and management practices.

Of course, it doesn't hurt to bring a passion for the arts to the mix. Many colleges offer programs that provide a good combination of both business and artistic training.

arts teacher Perhaps the job description for arts teachers (including drama, music, and art) should read something like "Wanted: experienced and talented art enthusiasts to inspire and guide a new generation of artists toward success and opportunity." That's because arts teachers are often so instrumental in uncovering artistic talent and empowering young artists to reach their dreams.

Like other kinds of teachers, arts teachers often favored their subject area before they were teachers. For instance, music teachers have often played in professional bands or orchestras. Drama teachers have usually acted in and directed theater productions. Art teachers are artistically gifted in one way or another. It's called life experience and it comes in especially handy when teaching art.

Sharing personal stories and experiences can be inspiring, but teaching demands a unique set of additional skills as well. Motivating students to work to their full potential tops the list. Drama teachers, for example, must get students to memorize lines, commit to after-school rehearsals, design sets, direct, and develop characters. In drama and other arts-related courses, traditional teaching methods like lectures and textbook-reading assignments sometimes just don't work, which can

Get Started Now!

Go to the head of the class and start a career in teaching:

- Take child development courses in high school.
- Do what you can to hone your artistic skills as an artist, dancer, actor, or musician by taking appropriate classes and participating in school and community-based arts programs.
- Volunteer to tutor younger students in after-school programs or consider applying for a part-time job at a child care center or summer day camp program to make sure that you enjoy spending lots of time with children.

Search It!

Educational Theatre Association at ***www.edta.org***, National Association for Music Education at ***www.menc.org***, and the Art Teacher Connection at ***www.artteacherconnection.com***

Read It!

Getty's ArtsEdNet at ***www.getty.edu/artsednet*** and the National Arts and Education Information Network at ***www.artsedge.kennedy-center.org***

Learn It!

- Bachelor's or master's degree in art, music, drama, or theater
- A state-licensing approved teacher education program

Earn It!

Median annual salary is $38,875. (Source: National Education Association)

Find It!

Arts teachers work at grade schools, high schools, and colleges. Visit the website of a district where you want to work.

Hire Yourself!

Pick a grade level (anywhere between kindergarten and high school). Pick a subject (art, dance, drama, or music). Pick a very specific topic within that subject (the field's wide open). Go on-line to Mid-Continent Research for Education and Learning (McRel) for background information (it's a resource that real teachers use): ***www.mcrel.org/lesson-plans/arts/index.asp***. Come up with a lesson plan that includes the topic, a description of what you want students to learn, and an outline of how you'll present the information. Be sure to include visuals and hands-on experiences as appropriate.

make teaching in the arts even more challenging—and interesting. Effective arts instruction often requires more of a "showing" than a "telling" approach.

Teaching, as you may have already noticed, has its perks. Summers off, with winter and spring breaks thrown in, probably top the list. And, believe us, you'll enjoy this benefit as much when you're a professional as you do now. Many teachers take advantage of that time to travel, develop new skills—and to recover from the stress of the school year. While teaching may seem like a breeze, it's demanding work for several reasons. First, teachers are essentially closed in a room with 20 or more children, teens, or adults—depending on the level at which they teach—for many hours a day. Then, there's prep time. Although it may be true that teachers only teach an average of six hours a day, it's not unusual for them to spend enormous amounts of time preparing lesson plans, grading papers, counseling students, and participating in extracurricular activities. The extracurricular part is especially true for arts teachers who may be involved in marching bands, choral concerts, theater productions, art exhibits, and the like.

But ask any truly committed teacher and, if it's a good day, he or she will tell you the benefits far outweigh the demands.

broadcast technician

Without broadcast technicians, there'd be no MTV, no hot new sitcoms, no crazy reality shows. Without these talented pros, your TV screens would be blank, and your radios would be silent. Long before the cameras roll or the music begins, broadcast techs are hard at work planning technical aspects of the show.

Most "techies" have a strong background in electronics and even a basic knowledge of electrical engineering. This technical expertise is generally applied to two main types of broadcasting functions: pushing the buttons and fixing the buttons.

"Button-pushers," or operators, run cameras, lights, videotape recording equipment, microphones, and the control boards that regulate the sounds and images being transmitted. Using computers, these technicians may also electronically alter and edit images or sounds. In a newscast, an operator brings up still images behind the announcer and types names beneath the image of the people being interviewed to identify them.

Get Started Now!

Get your career as broadcast technician on the air:

- Take any electronics or broadcasting classes offered at your school.
- Ask a teacher or guidance counselor to help arrange a tour of a local television or radio station.
- Volunteer to help with the operation of controls, microphones, and other equipment for your school's drama, music, sports, or broadcasting programs or at your place of worship.

Search It!
International Communications Industries Association (ICIA) at ***wwwinfocomm.org***, Society of Broadcast Engineers at ***www.sbe.org***, and AV Tech Online College Network at ***www.avtechonline.org***

Read It!
AV Video Multimedia Producer at ***www.avvmmp.com***

Learn It!

- Two-year or four-year degree in electrical engineering
- ICIA-approved training programs listed at ***www.avtechonline.org/AVTechOnline8.htm***

Earn It!
Median annual salary is $36,500. (Source: International Communications Industries Association)

Find It!
Most broadcast technician opportunities are with radio and television stations. Check out MTV at ***www.mtv.com*** and Clear Channel at ***www.clearchannel.com***.

Hire Yourself!

Take your pick. You are on the student board of directors for a prestigious professional association related to either broadcasting or audiovisual technology. You've been asked to give a presentation to a new group of student members about how any of the following equipment or technologies work:

- CDs
- Amplifier
- Analog/Digital recording
- Tape recording
- Movie sound
- Surround sound
- Microphones

A great place to start looking for information is the How Stuff Works website at ***www.howstuffworks.com***. Use your discoveries to prepare a 10-minute presentation for the new members. Find ways to integrate sound and visuals into your presentation using PowerPoint, posters, and boom box, or whatever tools are readily available to you.

The maintenance crew (or "button-fixers") makes sure the controls function properly. If there is a breakdown, they have to know how to fix things—and quick. If a radio or TV station stops broadcasting, it loses not only its audience, but also money from the advertisers whose commercials it should be airing. The job generally involves sitting in front of the controls in a temperature-controlled environment (which is needed to protect electronic equipment).

A closely related profession is audiovisual (AV) technician. AV techs are to live audiences (those who are actually present in an auditorium, conference center, or arena) what broadcast techs are to broadcast audiences (those who are listening to the radio in their cars or watching TV at home).

Tools of the trade for the AV profession include equipment such as amplifiers, sound boards, video screens, projectors, digital audio systems, and speakers. Of course, different types of presentations require different types of equipment. Some jobs require just a basic set-up—run some cable, flip a couple switches, and it's on with the show. Other productions, say something on the scale of a big name rock concert, can require upwards of 25 tons of equipment!

As technology advances, the required knowledge for technicians will become more advanced. Those interested in this career should be good at problem-solving and working with their hands. A background in algebra, advanced math, and physics can help with later technical training, and an artistic eye can actually benefit the technician who often must present images and sounds in an appealing way.

CAD (computer-aided design) technician

New roads, bridges, cell towers, or buildings actually get built twice. Once with brick, mortar, and cement, but first on a computer-aided design technician's computer screen. CAD technicians use computer-aided design software to create project models for engineering, construction, and architecture firms. Technology allows CAD techs or drafters, as they are also known, to accurately draw technical details such as specifications, codes, and calculations related to construction projects, equipment, or virtually any type of manufactured product you can imagine. CAD techs also use their skills to help manufacturers understand how their products will be constructed—whether the product in question is a car, a skateboard, a spacecraft, or a toaster. Even the boxes these products are packaged in were once conceptualized on a CAD tech's computer system.

CAD is most easily explained in the context of building. CAD techs use technology to help with everything from designing a skyscraper's exterior to charting the electrical plan in a mall. Because the work often incorporates drafting as well, the field is also referred to as CADD or computer aided design and drafting. CAD saves a lot of labor hours in the drafting process. Not long ago, drafters would take ideas, notes,

Get Started Now!

Design your career as a CAD technician:

- Take as much math, science, computer technology, computer design, and computer graphics as your schedule will allow.
- Test the waters by enrolling in one class in CAD at either a technical school or community college.

Search It!
The Association for Computer-Aided Design in Architecture at ***www.acadia.org*** and the American Design Drafting Association at ***www.adda.org***

Read It!
Cadalyst magazine at ***www.cadonline.com***

Learn It!

- Two-year degree from a technical college in engineering CAD technology
- Associate's degree from a community college in industrial draftng and CAD
- CAD technician certification program

Earn It!
Median annual salaries range from $36,000 to $42,000.
(Source: U.S. Department of Labor)

Find It!
CAD Technicians are often employed by architecture firms and engineering companies. Check out Stanley Consultants at ***www.stanleyconsultants.com***.

rough sketches, specifications, and calculations from engineers, architects, and designers and draw up construction designs in pen and ink (on what used to be known as the drawing board). They would have to draw and redraw plans countless times to get them right. Text was put on the page using stencils.

Now CAD technicians can swiftly produce walls, floors, lighting fixtures, windows, furniture, and plants on their computer screen. Moving items around and making changes simply require a few clicks of a mouse. With their computer keyboards and screens, technicians design with lines, circles, arcs, holes, slots, labels, pointers, markers, dimensions, and library symbols. The latest 3-D software makes computer models more realistic than ever. The technicians not only create the models that capture the vision of architects, but they also can translate the designs into working construction plans or blueprints that show exactly how tall each wall is and where each pipe will fit.

Many CAD technicians have some background in architecture and drafting. It can also be helpful to learn building codes. These codes often drive the work—for example, many CAD technicians redesign old structures to accommodate users with disabilities. They must know current code to draw in ramps and other universal access designs.

Anyone considering a future in CAD should have a strong foundation in science and math. Algebra and physics are especially helpful when considering how different forces come into play when building something. And of course prospective drafters should not only have excellent computer skills, they should also be able to draw freehand and they should be able to visualize in three dimensions.

Hire Yourself!

You've just completed training as a CAD technician. The best architectural firm in town is considering hiring you but wants to see if you've got the right stuff. They ask you, new grad that you are, to design the dorm room of the future using graph paper and pencil. Sketch your vision of the ideal dorm room, being sure to include the bed, bathroom, refrigerator, windows, closets, and bookshelves. (Note: If, by chance, you have access to computer-based design resources, please feel free to use them to complete this assignment.)

choreographer

"Five, six, seven, eight, and turn and kick and back to the beginning, people." Choreographers typically call out directions like that to guide dancers as they move their bodies with the rhythm of the music. In productions ranging from Broadway musicals like *Cabaret* or *Chicago* to music videos, these professionals are responsible for coordinating and developing the dance movements you see. Ballets, dance companies, television shows, films, and special events all rely on the art of the choreographer. Drawing on established forms of dance such as ballet, ballroom, tap, jazz, hip-hop, funk, and modern, dancing can tell a story, convey an idea, or set a mood.

A choreographed dance is a work of art. Before setting your sights on choreography, it's helpful, if not absolutely essential, to have a background in dance. Only someone who has danced extensively really understands how dancers work, their limitations and possibilities, and what motivates them. Plus, if you can perform the moves you create, you can better demonstrate them to others.

Get Started Now!

Get a move on now for a career in dance:

- Dance. Whether it's ballet, tap, jazz, modern, or folk—just do it!
- Join a competitive dance troupe or community theater group to get experience performing as a dancer.
- Rent movie musicals that demonstrate the works of famous choreographers—Bob Fosse (*Cabaret* and *Chicago*), Debbie Allen (*Flashdance*), and Hermes Pan (many Gene Kelly movies).

Search It!
National Dance Association at ***www.aahperd.org/nda***, Society of State Directors and Choreographers at ***www.ssdc.org***, and Dance USA at ***www.danceusa.org***

Read It!
Find advice for young dancers at ***www.danceusa.org/advice/high_school.htm*** and *Dance Magazine* at ***www.dancemagazine.com***.

Learn It!
- Bachelor's degree in dance and choreography
- Experience or an apprenticeship under an established choreographer

Earn It!
Median annual salary is $31,030. (Source: U.S. Department of Labor)

Find It!
Check out the Joyce Theatre at ***www.joyce.org***, Alvin Ailey at ***www.alvinailey.org***, and Snappy Dance Theater at ***www.snappydance.com***.

Hire Yourself

Ballet rules when it comes to dance. Almost all dance forms require at least a rudimentary knowledge of ballet. As the choreographer for a new children's ballet school, you want to make sure that your young students know the basics of ballet inside and out. Use websites such as ***www.nationalballetschool.org/pages/firststeps/index.html, www.ncdance.org/dance_101.htm, www.freewebs.com/variations/basics.html***, and other resources you find on-line or in the library to identify the five basic ballet positions and the seven movements of dance. Make a poster that you can use with your students to illustrate these important skills.

Like directors on a film, choreographers are take-charge types—they have to coordinate entire productions, organize and direct groups of people, and often handle administrative duties. They have to develop an authority and a unique vision that dancers will respect. To plan movements in advance, some tech-savvy choreographers now map out motions on the computer, while others draw storyboards, which can be helpful in plotting an elaborate piece.

Getting a presentation ready for a live audience requires intensive rehearsal. Rehearsals can go on for days, weeks, or even months. Needless to say, choreography is a career that demands a lot of energy and focus. It's a "people-person" job that not only requires team effort and good communication, but it can also require actual physical contact. They may work with large groups, solo artists, or couples (like a prima ballerina and her partner). They must understand how to cast the right dancers for each role and sometimes must decide on costumes, lighting, and music. Some choreographers even include spoken words and sound effects in their creations.

Many choreographers are retired dancers who want to remain active in the field. As with almost every job in the arts, choreographers are often freelance workers who may need to find additional means of financial support. Some are lucky to find positions as directors in residence with a production company, but others get part-time work teaching or coaching actors and dancers. Those who start their own companies have to become masters of marketing to sell their show to the public. Ultimately, success comes to those who are persistent, creative, and, in time, create their own unique style.

cinematographer

When the credits roll at the end of a major motion picture, look for the "director of photography." That's another title for cinematographer. It's the cinematographers's job to take thousands of perhaps seemingly random film clips and transform them into the kind of nonstop action and seamless stories that are hallmarks of a well-made film.

Cinematographers don't actually operate a camera—although most get their start working behind a camera. Their job blends endless amounts of creativity and technical know-how about light and cameras with impeccable organizational and management skills. Knowing how to coordinate the angles, lighting, and a crew of camera professionals often means the difference between a home video and a masterpiece. It's not as easy as it may sound. Good cinematographers develop a knack for seeing things that most people would never notice. And, oh, what a difference this keen sense of visual imagination can make to a film.

An interest in cameras and photography is often the prelude for a career like this. Photographers understand how to use light to change the moods in their photographs—and this same mastery of light applies to good filmmaking. Cinematographers also frame each shot as if it were

Get Started Now!

Get a career in cinematography rolling:

- Sign up for film design or multimedia courses offered at your school.
- Create your own home movies—concentrate on lighting and effectively capturing action.
- Join an after-school photography club or take a photography class—learning to take great photos is a first step toward becoming a cinematographer.

Search It!
American Society of Cinematographers at ***www.theasc.com***

Read It!
For the latest news in cinematography, go on-line to ***www.cinematographer.com***. For a crash course in filmmaking, go to ***www.learner.org/exhibits/cinema***.

Learn It!

- Bachelor's degree in film recommended
- For information, visit American Society of Cinematographers, ***www.theasc.com./resource/index.htm***

Earn It!
Median annual salary is $32,720. (Source: U.S. Department of Labor)

Find It!
Top film studios include Universal Studios at ***www.universalpictures.com*** and Miramax Films at ***www.miramax.com***. For a look at an educational approach to entertainment, try A&E's History Channel at ***www.thehistorychannel.com***.

Hire Yourself!

It's the chance of a lifetime. The Academy of Motion Picture Arts and Sciences needs your help in preparing a retrospective on Oscar-winning cinematography. Start with the Academy's database at ***www.oscar.com/legacy/pastwinners/cinema0.html*** and choose one winning movie representing each of the past five decades. Then do some Internet surfing and library research to find out all you can about each film. Fill a sheet of poster board with photocopies or computer printouts of pictures and informative captions that capture the essence of what made each film's cinematography especially great.

a "portrait in motion." The Tom Hanks film *Road to Perdition* was so beautifully filmed by the cinematographer Conrad Hall that critics have claimed that any single frame could hang on the wall as a work of art.

Keep in mind that most big-budget productions (and plenty of low-budget ones too) aren't limited to filming on sound stages on Hollywood's back lots. Some are filmed on location and require working around weather conditions, budget constraints, and local customs, if shot out of the country.

Think about any number of action films you've seen lately. It takes some fancy footwork to capture that kind of movement on film. That's why cinematographers need to know how to "dolly" a camera along tracks to keep pace with the action. Sometimes even a dolly isn't enough and scenes must be shot from above in a crane or even a helicopter. Other times, when actors are on the go, cameras are positioned in moving vehicles that move alongside the action.

Actually shooting the film is just the beginning of a cinematographer's work. After the film is shot, he or she must review the material and use sophisticated computer technology to edit and add special effects. This is a painstaking process and revered as an art form worthy of prestigious Academy Award (think Oscar) recognition.

Competition is stiff to work on major movies, but there's good news for up-and-coming cinematographers. Cable television, digital technology, and other advances are paving the way for increased opportunities with cable TV productions, commercials, educational programs, and low-budget independent films.

commercial artist

Think art. What's the first image that comes to mind? A work by one of the great masters? Picasso? Van Gogh? Dali? Warhol? Maybe the image involves a favorite CD cover, a funny poster, or that painting hanging over your family's fireplace. What does it take to produce memorable art? Maybe Ralph Waldo Emerson said it best when he said, "Artists must be sacrificed to their art. Like the bees, they must put their lives into the sting they give."

Artists use a wide variety of media to express their creativity, including painting, sculpture, pottery, photography, graphic design, and even yesterday's trash. Some artists create simply for the joy of creating; others create for both the pleasure and the pay, even though that pay may hardly cover the grocery bill. This is where the term "starving artist" sometimes comes in.

As the term "starving artist" implies, some artists barely scrape by. In order to make a living (great or small) creating art, artists must find someone to pay for their work. That somebody may be an art collector or it may be a company that produces and distributes a particular form of art such as pottery or postcards. The lesson here is that sometimes artists have to apply some creative energy to creating profitable avenues for their work.

Get Started Now!

Envision yourself as an artist:

- Take art classes to build your technique—learning the skills and tools of the artist can help bring your vision to life. Plus, the more you create, the better you get.
- Keep a sketchpad with so you can capture your ideas on paper whenever inspiration strikes.
- Visit art museums and art galleries every chance you get.

Search It!
National Endowment for the Arts at ***www.arts.endow.gov***

Read It!
Read about international art happenings and see artist portfolios at World Wide Arts Resources Corporation at ***www.absolutearts.com***.

Learn It!
Bachelor's or master's degree in fine art recommended

Earn It!
Median annual salary is $35,260. (Source: U.S. Department of Labor)

Find It!
Almost all fine artists are self-employed, but there are grants, foundations, patrons, and residency programs that help support the arts. Check out Arts and Healing Network at ***www.artheals.org/resource/grants*** and Moneyforart.com at ***www.moneyforart.com***.

Hire Yourself!

Only the world's greatest artists find their work exhibited at the National Gallery of Art. Go on-line to the Gallery's website at ***www.nga.gov/onlinetours/onlinetr.htm*** to find out for yourself why those artists made the cut. Take your pick of the on-line tours and in-depth study tours and create a display or presentation that answers the question "What's So Great about the Greats?"

For instance, one talented but unknown artist found a certain degree of fame and fortune when he traded putting his images on canvasses to putting them on sweatshirts and found upscale boutiques to sell his one-of-a-kind fitness clothing line. Another one found a way to pay the bills when he discovered a unique way to process photographs that gave them the appearance of a lithograph. With a little luck and lots of hard work, he found galleries all over the country that started snapping them up. Don't tell your parents, but more than one artist has created lucrative businesses designing and applying tattoos.

All this is not to say that it's impossible to make a living creating paintings, sculptures, and other "traditional" forms of art. Not at all. Anything is possible with exceptional talent, the right training, and the right connections. New York multimedia artist David Kramer is one success story. Not only has his art found an appreciative audience in the United States, but he's also making a splash abroad with successful shows in Canada and Europe. It all started when he was offered a paid residency in the Czech Republic where he met new artists who then recommended him to galleries in Europe and elsewhere. Another amazing success story features artist Liza Lou. She uses papier-mâché, fiberglass resin, wood, acrylic paint, and hundreds of thousands of glass beads to create incredible life-sized, three-dimensional depictions of everyday life. Her work has been featured in galleries around the world and exhibited at the Smithsonian American Art Museum.

Natural talent is, perhaps, more of a prerequisite for becoming an artist than it is for other types of occupations. However, being blessed with artistic flair does not preclude the need for formal training. Training options include a variety of fine arts or art history majors in college, studio apprenticeships, and specialized programs offered through museums such as Washington, D.C.'s Corcoran Gallery of Art and art institutes such as the San Francisco Art Institute.

corporate communications director

When McDonald's introduces a new and improved Big Mac, when Ford recalls an S.U.V., when Microsoft sponsors a charity program, it's their corporate communications director who gets the news outside the company to the media as well as inside the company to employees. It's their job to keep the lines of communication open and as friendly as possible.

As the title might suggest, keen communication skills are at the top of the list of requirements for this job. That means corporate communications directors know how to write and speak with accuracy and authority mixed with a certain degree of flair and panache and rounded off with the highest levels of professionalism and integrity. In many instances, the corporate communications director acts as the spokesperson for the company. Whether the news they're delivering is good or bad, their words and behavior must mirror a positive image that reflects well on the company.

Get Started Now!

Find your voice in corporate communications:

- Take speech, creative writing, and journalism courses in high school.
- Pay attention in your English composition and language arts classes. You will use every rule you encounter in these classes!
- Join the school debate team or volunteer to work on the school newspaper.

Search It!

The International Association of Business Communicators at ***www.iabc.com*** and the American Communication Association at ***www.americancomm.org***

Read It!

American Communications Journal at ***www.acjournal.org*** and the CW Bulletin at ***www.iabc.com/cw/public/index.htm***

Learn It!

- Bachelor's or master's degree in communications, journalism, or public relations
- A degree in any liberal arts subject that develops communications skills

Earn It!

Median annual salary is $60,640. (Source: U.S. Department of Labor)

Find It!

All major corporations employ communications directors. Look up your favorite companies on-line; fast food, fashion, or sports-related are good places to start.

Hire Yourself!

You're the communications director for your local school district. A well known snack food company has just offered to contribute a substantial amount of money to the district if the district will agree to allow the company to put its vending machines in all the district middle and high schools. The offer sounds too good to pass up. Or is it? The school superintendent has asked you to prepare a list of at least three pros and at least three cons regarding the benefits and potential problems associated with such a deal. Use the list to prepare a five-minute speech for the superintendent to present to the school board.

Tools that corporate communicators use to reach both internal (company employees) and external (the general public, investors, vendors, customers) audiences include resources like media releases, newsletters, websites, brochures, annual reports, multimedia presentations, and even bulletin board displays.

Strong and trustworthy communication is integral to the success of any corporation—so important that, in larger corporations, different communication jobs are often delegated to several departments, each tasked with specific communication goals. For instance:

- Community relations departments develop programs and activities that allow a company to give something back to the communities in which it operates. This might include organizing special events, volunteer programs, and charitable giving projects.
- Government relations departments monitor and influence legislation which affects the company or its products.
- Investor relations departments keep investors informed about the company's financial status by preparing quarterly and annual reports, coordinating shareholder meetings, and serving as the company's liaison with financial analysts and journalists.
- Corporate training departments provide in-house workshops and training sessions about topics as diverse as gender equity and disaster preparedness as well as keeping employees up to speed with new technological resources and specific job-related skills.

If you're good with words and people, this job can be an ideal match, and opportunities are expected to grow as corporations and media outlets continue to expand. Communications directors also find employment outside the corporate realm with hospitals, associations, the government, political groups, and universities.

costume designer

An actress appears on stage up to her chin in an elaborately ruffled collar attached to a floor-length gown made of yards and yards of the richest fabrics and festooned with a small fortune of jewels. The clothes convey an entitled sense of power, wealth, and prestige and you immediately accept the actress as Queen Elizabeth I who reigned over England from 1558-1603.

But, wait! You saw the same actress in a different movie just last week. In that role she was clad in mini-skirts and bikinis. Completely believable as a totally hip chick. So what gives? How can someone be accepted as a poster girl for Abercrombie and Fitch one week and some ancient queen the next?

It's all in the clothes. Costumes help establish the time period, as in a Civil War drama where uniforms and elaborate gowns bring the 1800s to life. They also help establish a character's personality and mood. Dark and mysterious garments certainly make villains seem more evil, and Superman without the tights and big red *S* on his chest would, well, definitely not be Superman. Think of how costumes help create the unique characters of *Harry Potter*, *Star Wars*, or the scarecrow, lion, and tin man in *The Wizard of Oz*.

As you may have guessed, all this imaginative wardrobing comes compliments of costume designers. Costume designers are part fashion designer, part history buff, part seamstress, part artist, part researcher, and

Get Started Now!

Take these steps to start a career in costume design:

- Sign up for clothing and design classes offered at your school.
- Join the school drama club and community theater group and volunteer to help with costuming.
- Go all out with your Halloween costume this year.

Search It!
Costume Society of America at ***www.costumesocietyamerica.com***

Read It!
Find a virtual costumer's library at ***www.costumes.org/pages/costhistpage.htm*** and links to all kinds of costume resources at ***www.costumedesign.net/research.html.***

Learn It!

- An education in fashion design and theater
- On-the-job training, working as assistant or volunteer
- Bachelor's or master's in fashion and/or theater design

Earn It!
Median annual salary is $29,200. (Source: U.S. Department of Labor)

Find It!
Theaters, movie studios, and multimedia corporations employ costume designers. Check out Disney Corporation at ***www.disney.go.com*** and HBO at ***www.hbo.com***

Hire Yourself!

Like virtually every high school in America, your school's drama department will be presenting an adaptation of Thornton Wilder's Pulitzer Prize-winning *Our Town*, a play about life and people living in Grover's Corners, New Hampshire. Presented in three parts, the play explores details about the town, the families and individuals who live there, love and marriage, and life and death. Although Wilder wrote the play in 1938, the play's themes are timeless. Your school's version of the play will take place in the same New Hampshire town in the 1970s. Your job is to create sketches (using colored pencils or pictures cut out of magazines or downloaded from a website) for three costume changes for four of the primary characters—George Gibbs and Emily Webb, neighbors and high school sweethearts who eventually marry; Doc Gibbs, George's father; and Mrs. Webb, Emily's mother. Websites to use for research include ***www.nhmccd.edu/contracts/lrc/kc/decade70.html***, ***www.fashion-era.com***, and ***www.costumegallery.com/1970.htm***. For additional resources, look for fashion history books in the library (and make copies of appropriate costumes), do your own Internet research, or, if all else fails, raid your parents' or grandparents' closet (with their permission, of course) to see if they have some oldies but goodies stashed away.

part accountant. They are responsible for either acquiring or creating all the costumes used in productions for film or stage—whether it's a major Broadway musical, a television sitcom, or a community ballet production.

Planning the costumes begins with a close reading of the script to get a complete sense of location, time period, and characters. Then, working closely with the director and keeping in mind a set budget, designers sketch the costumes for all the actors. Actors come in all shapes and sizes, so a familiarity with their physical attributes really helps in the design process.

As with any entertainment production, teamwork brings a drama to life. Designers collaborate with the set designers, make-up artists, and hair stylists to coordinate the overall look of a production. Because their materials are fabric and thread, costume designers must have core skills in sewing and reading patterns. As the characters in movies and plays have grown more exotic (think *The Lord of the Rings*), so have the costume materials. Today's designers need to know how to work with plastics, polymers, foam rubber, metals, and other materials to build elaborate creatures.

Production schedules often demand that designers work quickly and for long hours. They are typically hired as freelancers, contracted as non-staff workers for the duration of a production, although some are actually employed by motion picture studios or large theater companies. When a job ends, designers may devote a lot of time to searching for their next gig. They usually rely on a network of professionals and friends to find a new assignment. Organizations such as the United Scenic Artists Union (USAU) help independent designers survive. The USAU sets minimum fees and offers health and life insurance and a pension plan.

Beyond film and TV, opera companies, dance companies, and theme parks all hire costume designers. Considering that Walt Disney World alone maintains a working wardrobe of roughly 2.5 million costumes, there should be plenty to keep aspiring young costume designers busy.

Search It!
National Dance Council of America at ***www.ndca.org***

Read It!
Dance Magazine at ***www.dancemagazine.com***

Learn It!
- Training from a dance or ballet studio (with both competition and performance experience)
- Bachelor's or master's degree in dance

Earn It!
Median annual salary is $21,100. (Source: U.S. Department of Labor)

Find It!
Check out these major dance companies: Twyla Tharp Dance at ***www.twylatharp.org***, Mark Morris Dance Group at ***www.mmdg.org***, Colorado Ballet at ***www.coloradoballet.org***, and African American Dance Ensemble at ***www.africanamerican-danceensemble.org***. Check out ***www.dancecollective.com***, a career resource for dancers.

find your dancer future

dancer It's nothing new. Since the dawn of civilization, dancers have expressed ideas, stories, rhythm, and sound with their bodies. Dance is an art form where the artist is also the medium of expression.

When pursued as a profession, dance, like many other art forms, is much more than a way to make a living. It's a way of life—one that often starts in childhood and persists as long as the dancer's body will allow. While serious training for most careers begins after high school or college, many dancers are perfecting their moves by the time they're five years old and almost all by their early teens. Of course, it doesn't start as a calculated career plan. It generally starts as a pastime that becomes a passion.

Dancers are introduced to a variety of dance forms that allow free movement and self-expression, including classical ballet, modern dance, and culturally-specific dance styles.

To prepare for a professional career, dancers generally take one of two routes—either pursuing a college degree in dance or undergoing very rigorous and highly specialized dance training with a reputable dance company. College-level dance programs typically cover training in technique, composition, dance history, criticism, and movement analysis.

Dancers find work in a variety of places. Musical productions, operas, television shows, movies, music videos, and commercials are obvious performance outlets. However, dancers also take the stage onboard cruise ships, at dinner theaters, in entertainment theme parks, and in resorts. While the bright lights of Broadway in New York City lure many aspiring dancers, there are opportunities to be found in most big cities and in

Get Started Now!

Go through the motions of dance:
- Dance, dance, dance! At school, at a favorite dance studio, in community theater productions—wherever you can.
- Cultivate healthy nutritional and physical fitness habits.

a growing number of smaller ones. Other opportunities are found with dance companies that travel the country and even the world.

A couple of reality checks are advised for anyone considering a dancing career. First is the talent issue. If you don't have exceptional talent, you won't have a career. It's as simple—and as brutal—as that. Second is the age issue. Professional dancing is physically demanding work. Long years of practice and performance take their toll, and most dancers stop performing by their late thirties. While some remain in the field as choreographers, dance teachers, or artistic directors, others find themselves needing to find a second career. This, in itself, is not the end of the world. However, it's something to consider when planning a future in dance.

Hire Yourself!

It's time to chart your course as a dancer. Start with your first official dance class and create a timeline that showcases your training and dancing experiences so far. Use photos and descriptive words to add interest. All this information should be as accurate as possible.

Now comes the fun part. Use the second half of the timeline to map out your future as a dancer—as if the sky were the limit and wishes always came true. Indicate the kind of training you'd pursue and the kind of company you'd dance with. Complete your timeline with a fictional account of how your career might evolve beyond dancing.

Search It!
Association of Fundraising Professionals at ***www.afpnet.org*** and the Foundation Center at ***www.fdncenter.org***

Read It!
The *Chronicle of Philanthropy* at ***www.philanthropy.com***

Learn It!
- Bachelor's degree in nonprofit management, or arts management, business, or liberal arts
- Master's degree in fund-raising or public administration

Earn It!
Median annual salary is $56,000. (Source: Association for Fundraising Professionals)

Find It!
Visit sites for the Red Cross at ***www.redcross.org***, the Andy Warhol Foundation for the Visual Arts at ***www.warholfoundation.org***, and the Ford Foundation at ***www.fordfound.org*** for ideas. Find information about current opportunities at ***http://philanthropy.com/jobs***.

development director

Development directors, or fund-raisers, find creative ways to raise money for charitable causes. You love art, but you're not an artist. You love dance, but you're not a dancer. You love the theater, but you're not an actor. Here's a career where you can indulge your own passion while helping other artists indulge theirs.

It's important to note that this type of work is not limited to arts-related organizations. Generally speaking, development directors can work in hospitals and educational institutions, as well as nonprofit organizations related to everything from world peace to politics to music. Those with a passion for art find opportunities in art museums, art galleries, theater and dance companies, and regional and community performing arts organizations.

In a nutshell, a development director's main job responsibility is to find money to support his or her organization and its programs. How directors fulfill this obligation varies greatly and includes everything from direct mail efforts and special events (like charity balls, telethons,

Get Started Now!

Looking for a career where you can make a living by doing good? Try these first steps:

- Volunteer with an organization you believe in. Ask to work on telephone solicitations so you can have the experience of explaining a group's purpose and why it's so important to contribute.
- Join in a fund-raising drive at your school—a bake sale, car wash, raffle, etc.

Hire Yourself!

Believe it or not, your school is full of fund-raising opportunities. Parent/teacher organizations, booster clubs, sports teams, drama clubs, band—and the list goes on. Your job is to conduct a school-wide survey to find out how various groups are making money to support their causes. Prepare a chart that includes the group's name, a description of the fund-raising effort, and the amount of money raised. Look for trends associated with the most successful programs. Do an excellent job, share the results, and you can do lots of good right there in your own school.

and walkathons) to capital campaigns, product development and licensing, and grant proposals.

Grant writing is a key skill requirement for development directors. Many corporations, foundations, and wealthy individuals give away money to worthy causes. Getting the dollars, however, often requires submitting a grant proposal. That's why successful development directors know how to "talk" potential funders out of their money with a variety of relationship-building activities that include writing letters, preparing proposals, making presentations, and networking.

On the other side of the bucks are philanthropic individuals and organizations, foundations, and corporate community relations departments. Individuals in charge of money in these types of organizations are often called grants officers or community development directors, and are responsible for managing and disbursing funds designated specifically for good works.

On either side of the fence, whether asking for or giving money, a development director is someone with strong convictions who wants to make the world a better place.

Search It!
American Copy Editors Society at ***www.copydesk.org***, Youth Editors Association of America at ***www.naa.org/foundation/yeaa***, and ***www.copyeditor.com***

Read It!
Author Link at ***www.authorlink.com***

Learn It!
Bachelor's degree in journalism, communications, or English

Earn It!
Median annual salary is $41,170. (Source: U.S. Department of Labor)

Find It!
Visit Oxford University Press at ***www.oup.com***, Prentice Hall at ***http://vig.prenhall.com***, Hearst Publications at ***www.hearstcorp.com***, Ten Speed Press at ***www.tenspeedpress.com***, Globe Pequot Press at ***www.globe-pequot.com***, and Colorado Independent Publishers Association at ***www.cipabooks.com***.

editor Words are an editor's best friend—words found in manuscripts and proposals; words found in books, magazines, newspapers, or journals; words read by anchors on television and radio news broadcasts; and words churning out of every major corporation in the world.

Speaking of words, liaison is a good word to describe an editor's central role. Although they don't actually write books and articles, they work closely with the writers who do. Their involvement can be as broad as shaping the content of a new series of books or as narrow as refining a writer's style and repairing grammatical errors. In many ways, they represent the beginning and end of a book or article. They sort through sometimes endless piles of proposals and queries (called "slush piles") with a practiced and discerning eye toward discovering the next bestseller. They acquire the good ones, negotiate contracts with authors and writers, and help refine preliminary ideas into publishable concepts.

Another big editorial role comes into play when a manuscript or article is submitted for publication. That's when editors start the "fix-it" process by giving the material a careful and objective assessment.

Get Started Now!

Research a career in editing:

- Pay attention in your English literature and composition classes!
- Enroll in creative writing and journalism courses.
- Volunteer on the school newspaper, yearbook, or literary journal.
- Investigate internships that will give you hands-on experience in the publishing world. The American Society of Newspaper Editors lists newspaper internships nationwide (***www.asne.org/kiosk/careers/index.htm***) and the Mighty Internship Review lists all types of journalism internships (***www2.daily.umn.edu/~mckinney/indexwf.html***).

Hire Yourself!

It's the day you've been awaiting for a long time. You're part of the editorial team in charge of revising your least favorite high school textbook. You know the one. It was boring, hard to understand, and included graphics straight out of the Stone Age. Your job is to review the book with as much objectivity as you can muster while making two lists. The first list summarizes what you don't like about the current edition. The second list describes your recommendations for features that update the book in a way that provides interesting and effective learning experiences for high school students. Be prepared to present your opinions at the next editorial team meeting.

Relying on their knowledge of grammar, they patch up paragraphs with punctuation, smooth out bumpy passages, cut off repetitive phrases, and sharpen language to brighten up the occasional dull sentence.

People with a love for reading and writing are obvious choices for editorial work. And that doesn't necessarily mean they have to be devoted fans of Shakespeare and every book that was assigned in high school English Lit class. Editors apply their skills to publications ranging from college textbooks to comic books. Book and magazine editors are often experts in a particular subject—whether it's gardening, cooking, or mysteries.

Editors learn to evaluate manuscripts against the content needed to meet a publication's objectives and standards. For instance, editors at science magazines tend to have interests and awareness in that subject area. They understand what readers need and want to know about particular topics. When manuscripts are submitted, science editors have enough knowledge to evaluate a piece's accuracy (or are excellent fact checkers).

Editors also make sure that a story's "voice" is appropriate for its intended readers. Certainly an article written for a teenage fashion magazine will have a different style from a piece written for the *Wall Street Journal.*

If all this sounds like a big job, that's because it is. This is precisely why editorial duties in larger companies are disbursed among several types of editors:

- Editorial assistants handle the nitty-gritty details of the editorial office. (Truth be told, they generally get the tasks no one else wants or has time to do, but these positions are great learning experiences for someone new to publishing.)

- Editors are full-fledged project managers who work directly with authors and writers and others involved in the publishing process.
- Senior editors manage other editors within a department or division, and their work involves more administrative duties such as long-range planning, budgets, and sales projections.
- Acquisitions editors seek out and sign new projects and writers to add to their publisher's "list."
- Copy editors are ultimately responsible for ensuring that publications go to print in tip-top shape.
- Editor in chief is a job title most often associated with newspapers and magazines and is pretty much what the name implies—the boss of all the editors—and chief decision maker about content included in each issue.

Jobs for editors are wide ranging. Wherever there are written words in abundance, editors are needed—for press releases, websites, political speeches, medicine instructions, equipment manuals, and books like the one you're reading.

Search It!
International Association of Clothing Designers (IACD) at ***www.iacde.com/english/index.htm***

Read It!
Elle, Vogue, Harper's Bazaar, or other fashion magazines, and *Fashion Planet* at ***www.fashion-planet.com***

Learn It!
- Bachelor's degree in fashion design or fashion merchandising
- Look for schools at the National Association of Schools of Art and Design at ***www.arts-accredit.org/nasad/pur.html***

Earn It!
Median annual salary is $51,290. (Source: U.S. Department of Labor)

Find It!
Gain experience working for name designers, such as Donna Karan (***www.donnakaran.com***) and Calvin Klein (***www.macys.com***), or major retailers such as Gap (***www.gap.com***) or Urban Outfitters (***www.urbanoutfitters.com***).

fashion designer

One of the most amazing things about the work of a fashion designer is that you see it everywhere. Just look in the mirror and there it is. Look at what your friends are wearing and there it is again. Look at what your parents are wearing and there it is again—although almost certainly by a different designer.

A creative fashion designer created the low-ride pants, tank tops, the bell bottoms so popular at the turn of the 21 st century (and also when your parents were young). Are these styles still popular? Fashion designers have to be keenly aware of what's hot and what's not, because their livelihoods depend on producing clothes people will pay to wear at a given place and time. Fashion trends can be fleeting. What's in one day can be out the next. The best fashion designers seem to develop an almost uncanny ability to stay a step ahead of the fashion police.

Make no mistake, however—fashion design is an art form. People are the canvas and their clothes are the medium. Fashion designers know how to create patterns, cut materials, drape and sew fabrics—all in the common pursuit of making people of all shapes and sizes look good.

Fashion designers draw on a deep knowledge of all fabrics—cotton, wool, polyester, latex, silk, and others—to envision their own designs. Many have extensive knowledge of fashion history and current styles (thanks to a well-rounded education) so they can draw on both the past and present to develop their new fashion directions.

Get Started Now!

Design your future:
- Take clothing and design courses at school.
- Enroll in special classes offered at local fabric stores, craft centers, or community art programs.
- Cultivate an eye for fashion by regularly perusing fashion magazines.

Hire Yourself!

Portfolios are a must-have accessory for fashion designers everywhere. Here's a project to get some experience—only this time you can use other people's work. Use fashion magazines, catalogs, and websites to gather a collection of photographs that illustrate fashion trends in your school. Make sure to fill at least four pages and include descriptive captions that at least attempt to explain the fashion statements being made by your classmates.

Ideas begin with detailed sketches, using such elements as zippers, buttons, cuffs, hoods, or fringes that are useful and/or decorative. When an idea is finalized, the designer pulls out scissors and thread and creates a sample garment to see how it fits on a mannequin or live model. The designer keeps careful records of dimensions, color schemes, and materials.

For top fashion designers, a unique combination of vision and business savvy have made many of them household names—like Versace, Armani, and Tommy Hilfiger. Designers like these are important players in the high-stress, high-profile world of high fashion that culminates in famous Paris and New York runway fashion shows. Their names sell clothes and are attached to multimillion-dollar businesses.

Only a small percentage of designers make it to these lofty heights. Many other designers sell their originals from small boutiques or mass market them through department stores. Still others are employed by certain fashion labels or fashion chain stores like Abercrombie and Fitch and Banana Republic.

Fashion has many niche areas. Some designers thrive on producing garments specifically for babies, wedding parties, or large-size customers. Beyond clothes, designers create towels, sheets, luggage, jewelry, and other accessories. Others design fabric and furniture.

The first step for any designer is building a portfolio that showcases designs and samples of work. For a beginner, nothing beats experience. College fashion design programs often provide experience through co-op education that puts students to work part time in the fashion industry.

film director

There's nothing quite like going to see a good movie or play. When done right, everything seems so real. The acting appears effortless; the scenes flow together seamlessly. It's as if viewers are transported into another place and time. Entertainment like this doesn't just happen. It takes someone behind the scenes pulling everything together to make it happen. That someone is the director.

Directors are the driving force behind every movie, television show, or theatrical production. Compare a production to a ship and the director is the captain. Compare it to a corporation and the director is the boss. While the job requires many skills, two, in particular, top the list—organization and creativity.

Directors don't work alone. They work with a team of highly trained professionals that includes actors, producers, technical directors, cinematographers, and a host of others. But directors are probably best known for directing actors. Scene after scene, directors monitor every word, every movement, every sound—offering advice and guidance at every step of the process. The same scene can be rehearsed and shot dozens and even hundreds of times before satisfying the director. Good directors know how motivate their actors and how to draw deep and emotionally rich performances from them.

Get Started Now!

Want to develop a sense of direction? Try the following:

- Get involved in school or community theater productions. Volunteer to assist the teacher or director to get a firsthand look at what it takes to pull a play together.
- Pretend you're a movie critic and watch as many movies and plays as possible. Evaluate the acting, the lighting, the sound, the editing, and all the elements that went into the production.

Search It!
Directors Guild of America at ***www.dga.org***

Read It!
Videomaker at ***www.videomaker.com*** and DirectorsWorld at ***www.uemedia.com/CPC/directorsworld***

Learn It!
Bachelor's degree in filmmaking, multimedia production, or technical theater

Earn It!
Median annual salary is $56,090. (Source: U.S. Department of Labor)

Find It!
Find links to major and independent film companies, including 20th Century Fox, Columbia Pictures, and DreamWorks, at ***www.mainstwebdesign.com/link_library/film-studios.htm***.

Hire Yourself!

Document your life. Get a film or video camera and make a brief documentary about some part of your life. It could be about a sport you love, your family, your girlfriend or boyfriend, your pet, your town. Think it through before you start aiming the camera. Prepare a script and plan the sequence of action to tell a compelling story.

In addition to the actors, every film or play involves a staff of technical experts that is managed by the director. Planning a movie or play begins with set designers, costume designers, and casting agents. Artists draw out storyboards that resemble panels in a comic book and outline the series of actions and sets to be filmed.

During the actual filming or rehearsals, the director confers with the cinematographer, lighting director, and sound technicians to make sure all the scenes are being properly captured on film. After the filming is over, directors work with film editors, composers, and special effects experts to create the final cut. Coordinating such a circus of activity is a big job and requires lots of skill and confidence.

Adding to the breathless pace, filmmakers often must travel from studio sets to different locations. To create the mythical world of *The Lord of the Rings*, director Peter Jackson filmed mostly in the forests and mountains of New Zealand.

The number of opportunities continues to grow for directors as cable TV, educational programming, and the Web expand. Live theater may provide fewer opportunities and less pay than working in film or television, but it's often a good training ground for future filmmakers. Those wanting to break into the business often make their own independent features. Fortunately, the filmmaking process has become a little bit less expensive because of new digital technology. To gain experience, budding directors often start in lesser roles—production assistants, assistant directors, and cinematographers.

Film director Guillermo del Torro gave this advice to young filmmakers: "Do it as often as you can. Regardless of how cheap or silly your little movies look, or video, you will be gaining practice. At the end of the day, that counts a lot."

graphic designer

Graphic artists work at the crossroads of art and commerce. They use art to help sell—in magazines, on billboards, and on the Internet. They generate corporate logos and product packaging. Take a close look at that soda can you're holding—its design originated in the mind of a graphic artist. The work can be as simple as a poster announcing a storewide sale or as detailed as an annual report for a major corporation. For a magazine article, designers want to attract readers with dynamic combinations of words and graphics.

No matter what the design, most graphic designers depend on computer technology using programs such as Quark and Photoshop to create their masterpieces. Sitting in front of large computer monitors, they manipulate typefaces, photos, and other artwork to produce appealing material. For Web and CD-ROM designs, professionals rely on programs that create moving images and sound. Occasionally, designers will even blow the dust off their pen and paper and produce art directly by hand.

To get into this career, you have to know some art basics—illustration, design, painting, and typography. A background in art history is

Get Started Now!

Design your future.

- Start to learn how to use some basic computer design software at your high school, a computer training center, an art and design school, or community college.
- Work on the layout of the school newspaper, literary magazine, or yearbook.
- Make it a habit to buy magazines (or read them in the library) and look at them with an eye for the design. How are type and art or photography combined to give an article punch?

Search It!
American Institute of Graphic Arts at ***www.aiga.org*** and Graphic Artists Guild at ***www.gag.org***

Read It!
Graphic Arts Monthly at ***www.gammag.com***; *Communication Arts* magazine at ***www.commarts.com***

Learn It!
- Associate's or bachelor's degree in graphic design
- Browse a list of schools at ***www.graphicdesignschoolreview.com***

Earn It!
Median annual salary is $36,680. (Source: U.S. Department of Labor)

Find It!
Many graphic designers work for magazines, or public relations or advertising firms. Visit Hearst Publishers at ***www.hearstcorp.com***, G & J USA Publishing at ***www.gjusa.com***, and AOL Time Warner at ***www.aoltimewarner.com***.

Hire Yourself!

Wow! Your favorite band is coming to town. Knowing you're such an ardent fan, they've agreed, at the last minute, to do a special performance at your high school. There isn't much time to get the word out. Your job is to design a poster that can be copied and posted all over the school and throughout the community. Start by downloading a photo of your favorite group from the Internet. Then, depending on available resources and your current skills, use either a computer program like Microsoft Publisher or colored markers to create a poster that will fill the auditorium with fellow fans.

helpful for inspiration and techniques. To better understand how art can sell, designers can benefit from courses in merchandising, business management, marketing, and psychology.

One essential talent for this job is almost impossible to learn: aesthetic sense. You either have it or you don't. Those who have the talent know what colors look good together, how a design is balanced and proportional, and what is beautiful to the eye. They simply see things in ways that others don't.

Before any design is seen by the public, a big group effort has gone into it. Typically, graphic designers work closely with clients to make sure the message is clearly defined and to conceptualize the visual direction. Based on client input, designers determine shape, color, materials, and costs. The process of making a vision a reality may require close work with writers, layout artists, production artists, illustrators, photographers, and printers. Often the work must be completed under tight deadlines to meet production schedules.

When hunting for employment in this field, a good resume is needed, but a great portfolio will ultimately land the job. A portfolio contains samples of the designer's best work and demonstrates versatility and originality. Fresh ideas are what sell, so designers must continually stay on top of new looks and trends.

find your illustrator future

illustrator If you've got the "art" stuff and are thinking about making art your career, illustration is an option you'll want to consider. While the work of some fine artists who create paintings and sculptures is driven by more personal inspiration, illustrators tend to create art for very specific commercial purposes. Their drawings complement magazine articles, decorate cereal boxes, adorn book jackets, accompany birthday card greetings, sell products from billboards, and announce movie openings on posters. Just about everywhere you look, you'll see the work of an illustrator.

The most successful illustrators develop distinct and recognizable styles—a process that takes lots of practice. The late Al Hirschfeld, for example, was known as the "Line King" and is renowned for his drawings of celebrities. Driven by imagination and creativity, illustrators traditionally work directly on paper with paints, inks, and pencils. Some illustrators specialize in collage, pasting different cutout bits together to form a whole image. Others use computer technology to create their work. No matter the original process, virtually all illustrations used in professional publications end up in a computer system where they are converted into digital files that can readily be used and manipulated by graphic designers and printers.

Get Started Now!

Line up a career in illustration:

- Take art classes in high school. Ditto on computer design courses.
- Volunteer your talents for the school newspaper, yearbook, and literary magazine.
- Don't leave home without your sketchbook. Draw everything you see, every chance you get. The more you draw, the better you will get.

Search It!
The Society of Illustrators at ***www.societyillustrators.org***, the Illustration Conference at ***www.theillustrationconference.org***, and the Illustrator's Association at ***www.illustrators.org***

Read It!
Communication Arts magazine at ***www.commarts.com***

Learn It!

- Associate's or bachelor's degree in fine art or illustration
- The Society of Illustrators lists schools at ***www.societyillustrators.org***

Earn It!
Median annual salary is $35,260. (Source: U.S. Department of Labor)

Find It!
For magazines, visit *Rolling Stone* at ***www.rollingstone.com*** or *Entertainment Weekly* at ***www.ew.com***; for children's books, Scholastic at ***www.scholastic.com***; for greeting cards, Hallmark at ***www.hallmark.com***.

Hire Yourself!

A community youth center has announced that they want to create a mural in the new gymnasium that reflects the best things about your hometown. They've invited young local artists (like you) to submit a sketch illustrating their best ideas. Make a list of the people, places, and things that make your town unique. Then create a sketch that incorporates these ideas in a creative and memorable way.

When drawing for a specific magazine article, an illustrator may have to read the piece and come up with a few different sketches that will capture the theme of the piece. He or she may consult with an art director on the layout and discuss possible concepts. Once the illustrator submits sketches, the art director may ask for revisions.

Almost all illustrators work for themselves, so some business know-how is vital. Illustrators need to understand how to estimate job costs, negotiate fees, sign agreements, and produce invoices. Because publications often want to reprint work, they often negotiate for reprint fees. They sometimes turn to organizations such as the Graphic Artists Guild for help in developing business standards and other professional development. To get jobs, illustrators build a portfolio of their best work and then present it to prospective employers.

This is a very competitive field, but some illustrators thrive by specializing in a particular area, such as medical illustration or children's books. Ultimately, those who succeed are dedicated to developing their technique, persevere in the search for assignments, and continually maintain professionalism.

interior designer

Cable television shows about interior decorating are wildly popular, and newsstands are stuffed with magazines about home improvement. You may have even heard talk about feng shui, an ancient Chinese art based on the idea that how you arrange your living space can lead to emotional and spiritual harmony. (Check ***www.fengshuisociety.org.uk***.) People everywhere are actively seeking ways to make their home and work spaces functional and great looking—and that may explain why interior designers are in big demand.

Interior designers make life more beautiful. According to the American Society for Interior Designers, they are qualified to "enhance the function and quality of interior spaces by education, experience and examination." It's all done for the purpose of "improving the quality of life, increasing productivity, and protecting the health, safety and welfare of the public."

People's homes are, of course, the first place to look for evidence of an interior designer's work. However, interior designers apply their skills to improve the physical environment of everything from business offices and industrial workplaces to all manner of transportation includ-

Get Started Now!

Plan a career in interior design:

- Enroll in any interior design courses offered at your school.
- Visit local furniture, fabric, and accessory stores to get a sense of the latest decorating trends.
- Go to a home and garden trade show. Interior designers usually exhibit at these shows, which are typically held at civic centers in major metropolitan areas.
- Work on a home improvement project with your parents or family.

Search It!
American Society for Interior Designers at ***www.asid.org*** and International Interior Design Association at ***www.iida.org***

Read It!
ISdesigNET at ***www.isdesignet.com*** and interior design books and magazines

Learn It!

- Associate's or bachelor's degree in interior design
- The Foundation for Interior Design and Research lists accredited programs at ***www.fider.org***

Earn It!
Median annual salary is $39,180. (Source: U.S. Department of Labor)

Find It!
Visit *Trading Spaces* at ***www.tlc.discovery.com***, Home and Garden TV at ***www.hgtv.com***, and the Hickory Furniture Mart at ***www.hickoryfurniture.com***.

Hire Yourself!

It's time to give your room a makeover! Use pictures from magazines and color samples from paint stores, fabric stores, and carpet stores to create a collage that illustrates the room you'd love to come home to. The only constraint is that you must work within the actual space of your current bedroom. Set a budget and see how much flair you can create in your room while pinching your pennies at the same time.

ing trains, ships, airplanes, submarines, and spaceships. They also create the ambience found in restaurants, hotels, resorts and spas, retail stores, and malls, and they develop designs to meet the unique requirements of churches, synagogues, and other places of worship. Believe it or not, even government agencies and schools get spruced up under the care of interior designers.

Good taste, while useful in interior design, is not the final word. Success in interior design is more a matter of a designer's ability to interpret what the client wants. There are so many choices and styles to use in decorating spaces—traditional, contemporary, postmodern, and French country to name a few. Then there are practical considerations about how the space is to be used. The most dazzling design work is of no use if it's not functional and well-suited to its purposes. And, of course, there are almost always budget constraints to work with (or around). Sometimes the sky's the limit, but more often it takes every creative idea and frugal resource a designer can muster to keep a budget in check. Tune in to any number of popular interior design shows on Home and Garden TV channel (see ***www.hgtv.com*** for local listings) for real-life examples of how this process works.

The real test comes after the designer has crafted winning ideas and actually implements the plan. The implementation phase can include everything from finding a precise shade of paint and chasing down just the right antique accessory to using special computer programs to sketch out furniture arrangements and contracting with painters, builders, furniture designers, and other craftspeople to bring designs to life. Everything comes together with a carefully balanced mix of artistic skill, keen attention to detail, and people-pleasing skills.

Professional training is a must for a career in interior design, with most positions requiring a two- or four-year degree in interior design. A good college or technical school program is where designers gain the knowledge and skills to perform tasks involving design analysis, space planning, and building codes, and to master design-related computer programs. As is true of many creative occupations, training continues throughout a designer's career in the form of workshops, self-guided learning programs, and seminars.

Although much time is spent sitting at a desk planning, sketching designs, and seeking out suppliers, the job can get physical when professionals do the hands-on work of implementing designs, which can involve anything from climbing ladders to paint and hang drapes to getting down and dirty to lay carpets and arrange furniture.

Self-employment is one route chosen by interior designers. Others seek employment in design and architectural firms and retail stores. However, in-house design opportunities can be found in some rather unexpected places such as museums, amusement parks, health care facilities, and real estate companies.

Search It!
Society of Professional Journalists at ***www.spj.org***, American Society of Journalists and Authors at ***www.asja.org***, the Dow Jones Newspaper Fund at ***http://djnewspaperfund.dowjones.com***

Read It!
The Journalist's Road to Success at ***http://djnewspaperfund.dowjones.com/fund/pubcareerguide.asp*** and the *American Journalism Review* at ***www.newslink.org***

Learn It!
- Associate's or bachelor's degree in journalism or mass communication
- Master's degree in journalism

Earn It!
Median annual salary is $30,510. (Source: U.S. Department of Labor)

Find It!
Investigate the Gannett newspaper chain at ***www.gannett.com***, *Newsweek* magazine at ***www.newsweek.com***, CNN at ***www.cnn.com***, and the on-line magazine *Slate* at ***www.slate.msn.com***.

journalist

Never before in the history of mankind have journalists done so much to bring late-breaking, up-to-the-minute news to virtually every home and office in the developed world. Wars are won and lost in full living color. Heartbreaking tragedies (who will ever forget seeing the Twin Towers crumble on 9/11?) and awe-inspiring triumphs are broadcast all over the world within nanoseconds of their occurrence. All this is possible because journalists are on the scene wherever and whenever news is happening—which sometimes translates into long hours, great personal sacrifice (think war zones), and challenging situations.

When all is said and done, journalists are truth-seekers. They are motivated by a need to understand how the world works and to share what they learn with the public. Many write about current events that affect our lives—whether they occur on a local, national, or global level. If there is a fire at a nightclub, journalists give the details of how it started and who was injured. If the President presents a tax-cut program, reporters explain how it impacts the average taxpayer, doing their best to present an objective and balanced story.

Get Started Now!

Develop a nose for news:

- Get involved in reporting for your school paper. Find inspiration and samples of school newspapers from around the country at the American Society of Newspaper Editors's high school journalism website at ***www.highschooljournalism.org.***
- Seek out internship opportunities. Find opportunities at the American Society of Newspaper Editors websites at ***www.asne.org/kiosk/careers/index.htm.***

Hire Yourself!

Follow that story. Look at the front page of a current edition of a major newspaper. Pick a major story of interest and cut it out. Now go on-line to websites like ***www.cnn.com***, ***www.msnbc.com***, ***www.nytimes.com***, and ***www.washingtonpost.com***. Find coverage about the same story and print out related articles. Read each story carefully and make a chart comparing the key points and conclusions made in each article. For extra credit, check the same stories one week later and take note of any changes in prominence (are stories buried in the back of the paper or still front page news?) and circumstances.

In many ways, journalists keep the world honest as well. Investigative journalists look into the practices of major corporations. An electrical power company should know that if it dumps hazardous waste into a local river, a journalist is sure to find out and expose it to the public. Politicians are well aware that their careers can end if an ever-vigilant journalist discovers they've been involved in any criminal activity (as former President Nixon found out). Freedom of the press is a precious safeguard, allowing journalists to tell what powerful people would sometimes rather keep hidden from the public.

As you might expect, at their very core, journalists are wordsmiths. They know how to use language effectively to communicate. The skills they develop depend on the medium they pursue—a newspaper reporter focuses on the written word while broadcasters are more concerned with the spoken word.

Writing articles demands long hours gathering information, often interviewing dozens of people to build a comprehensive, balanced work. (Students who enjoy doing research on school papers under tight deadlines may find the career is a perfect match.) Journalists must be comfortable talking with people, often asking them difficult questions about sensitive issues. To record the information, journalists find it helpful to be quick note-takers.

Typically, journalists narrow their focus and become specialists—writing about business, technology, health, education, sports, or entertainment, for example. Scientific and technical reporting are two areas that are expected to be hot throughout this decade. Although it's a competitive field, opportunities are everywhere. Journalists work in small towns on local newspapers and in big cities at major television networks. As the worlds of cable television and the Internet continue to grow, so will the need for ace reporters.

Search It!
The International Alliance of Theatrical Stage Employees at ***www.iatse.lm.com***, Entertainment Services and Technology Association at ***www.esta.org***, and United States Institute for Theater Technology, Inc. at ***www.usitt.org***

Read It!
Resources found at ***www.controlbooth.com***

Learn It!
- Associate's, bachelor's, and master's degrees in technical theater
- Learn about apprenticeships at ***www.iatse.lm.com/stgtrain***

Earn It!
Median annual salary is $39,565. (Source: U.S. Department of Labor)

Find It!
The top movie studios, television stations, and theaters employ lighting technicians. Look into Disney at ***www.disneyworld.com***, Fox at ***www.fox.com***, and Castle Rock Entertainment at ***www.castle-rock.warnerbros.com***.

lighting technician

Lights! Camera! Action! Those are the words traditionally called out by the director as filming begins and cameras roll. The first word points out how important it is to have the proper lights in a movie production. Providing illumination is the responsibility of the lighting technicians. These experts use lights to enhance the moods and atmosphere in live theater, film, television, and other staged events such as rock concerts.

Sometimes called juicers or gaffers, lighting technicians set up lights, direct them on the action, and operate the boards that control them. In a studio, lights may be set up in the ceiling in an elaborate grid that is controlled from a central control panel or booth. The job requires a unique combination of visual creativity, technical know-how, and physical stamina.

To create art with light, these specialists use colored tints, filters, light patterns, black lights, and controls to fade light up or down. On the technical end, these experts understand basic principles of how to handle electricity. When we plug in a lamp at home, we tend not to think of how dangerous electricity can be. But these professionals often deal with heavy power loads and all the wires needed to accommodate lots of light—so safety is an important issue.

Get Started Now!

A career as lighting technician does not need to be light years away:

- Assist behind the scenes in a school or local theater production.
- Rent movies and carefully observe how scenes are lit and how the atmosphere changes as the lighting changes. Critique scenes on how well-lit they are (or aren't).
- Look into training programs to become an electrical technician—community colleges are often a good place to start.

Hire Yourself!

The technical theater department of your community's playhouse needs a how-to guide for its behind-the-scenes technical staff and has hired you to put one together. Use resources and information you find at the following websites (and any you find using your favorite Internet search engine) to compile a useful training notebook for lighting technicians, grips, and gaffes.

- Stage Specs Online at ***www.stagespecs.com***
- Technical Theater at ***www.technicaltheater.com***
- Cinematography Resource Links at ***http://cinematography.com/links***
- Backstage Web at ***www.backstageweb.com/links.htm***
- Biggest Theater Glossary on the Web at ***www.theatrecrafts.com/glossary/glossary.html***

Make sure to include descriptions and photos as well as a glossary of common terms.

When equipment malfunctions or short-circuits, the lighting crew springs to action and makes repairs with screwdrivers, pliers, wrenches, and gloves for handling hot bulbs. The art of lighting has become more sophisticated as computers are now used to automate functions. Lights can now change on cue during a performance without technicians lifting a finger. Lighting knowledge can get even more complicated on specialized shoots, such as underwater filming or nature documentaries.

Technicians who are not in shape when they begin get in shape fast. The job demands moving heavy lights, lighting stands, wires, and cables. Generators often have to be hauled to sets on location. Because bulbs are often high up in ceilings, technicians climb up tall ladders to make adjustments and fixes. They can't be afraid of heights!

All entertainment productions are exercises in teamwork. Lighting technicians work closely with the director and set designer to produce the desired effects. On a film they consult with the cinematographer, whose biggest concern is having enough light to capture the action on film.

Besides those who specialize in lighting, there are many other technicians in the entertainment industry—special effects experts, key grips, production assistants, electricians, and sound technicians, to name a few. Most have to work in the entertainment capitals—New York and Los Angeles—but there are opportunities in other major metropolitan areas such as Atlanta, Miami, Las Vegas, and Chicago.

lobbyist

As representatives of major corporations and organizations, lobbyists employ the powers of persuasion to influence the decisions of government officials on the local, state, and national levels. Lawmakers have the power to enact legislation that can impact specific industries or nonprofit groups in huge ways—for good or for bad.

Lobbyists who get results possess exceptional communication skills—of both the written and verbal varieties. They are able to address issues confidently because, frankly, they do their homework. For instance, a lobbyist working on behalf of AIDS research would know the issue inside out. They'd understand the nature of the disease and its effect on infected people throughout the world. They'd review existing legislation and identify gaps in services and resources. They then would use all this information to develop well-articulated arguments to present either in favor of or against new legislation under consideration, or in some cases, to initiate support for new legislation.

Lobbyists must be experts about their particular issue and use their knowledge (and opinions) to inform government officials and other key decision-makers. This is especially important in light of the fact that legislators on both state and national levels are often asked to consider thou-

Search It!
The American League of Lobbyists at ***www.alldc.org***, the American Association of Political Consultants at ***www.theaac.com***, and the American Political Science Association ***www.apsanet.org***

Read It!
"Lobbying as a Career" at ***www.alldc.org/career.htm***

Learn It!
- Bachelor's or graduate degree in political science, history, public relations, nonprofit management, government relations, or political management
- Browse a list of graduate programs at ***www.theaapc.com/content/resources/links.asp***

Earn It!
Median annual salary is $39,600. (Source: U.S. Department of Labor)

Find It!
Corporations and nonprofit organizations hire lobbyists, such as the AFL-CIO at ***www.aflcio.org***, the Sierra Club at ***www.sierraclub.org***, and Shell Oil at ***www.shell.com***.

Get Started Now!

Need any convincing to be a lobbyist? Try these steps:
- Take courses in government, speech, and debate.
- Get involved in student government or student council at your school.
- Volunteer to help a candidate during a local, state, or national election.
- Consider pursuing a Congressional internship while in college. Find information at ***www.politixgroup.com/dcintern/congress.htm.***

Hire Yourself!

No matter the cause, understanding the legislative process is one thing all lobbyists need to do. Your job, as a future lobbyist, is to figure out how laws are made. Get the federal lowdown at ***http://thomas.loc.gov/home/lawsmade.toc.html*** and use the Internet to find additional information as needed. Use what you've found to create a chart that illustrates the process in simple, step-by-step terms that even a child (or a newly elected politician) could understand.

sands of bills during a legislative session (a period of time that varies but generally lasts from one to six months). There is no way that legislators can fully research every issue themselves. They depend on lobbyists to help them make informed decisions.

This brings up a very important point about a very important issue—trust. Success as a lobbyist is largely a matter of earning trust and keeping it. It's no secret that many lobbyists are paid to look out for their employer's self interests. Others work on behalf of special-interest groups such as colleges, churches, and senior citizen organizations. Long-term credibility as a lobbyist requires building solid relationships with government decision-makers. These kinds of relationships, as is true of most good relationships, require the kind of mutual respect that comes from honest and fair dealings. Just in case someone tries to abuse the system, there are strict laws and stiff penalties safeguarding the lobbying process.

Lobbying often involves very intense work (which, coincidentally, is what draws so many talented people to the field). Whenever a relevant issue is up for grabs, lobbyists closely monitor the legislative process as new bills and laws are developed in committees and work their way through the system toward legislative votes. Lobbyists use a variety of techniques to accomplish their goals including meeting one-on-one with legislators, hosting policy forums and symposiums, developing reports and public information campaigns, and sometimes even organizing coalitions of like-minded organizations and galvanizing community action groups.

By the way, the term "lobbyist" has an interesting history. President Ulysses S. Grant used to escape the pressures of the White House by spending evenings in the lobby of the nearby Willard Hotel where many would-be power brokers approached him on individual causes. According to historians, it was President Grant himself who coined the phrase by calling these people "lobbyists."

Search It!
American Association of Museums at ***www.aam-us.org***

Read It!
Museum News at ***www.aam-us.org/pubp.htm***

Learn It!
- Master's degree in art history or museum studies generally required
- Master's or Ph.D. degree in the subject one wishes to curate
- Undergraduate degree in history or library science

Earn It!
Median annual salary is $35,270. (Source: U.S. Department of Labor)

Find It!
All museums need curators—check out the American Museum of Natural History at ***www.amnh.org***, the Art Institute of Chicago at ***www.artic.edu***, the National Gallery of Art at ***www.nga.gov***, and ***www.museumstuff.com/showcase***.

museum curator

If you've ever collected anything—stamps, bugs, baseball cards, bellybutton lint—you may have a natural inclination toward being a museum curator. Especially if you're the type of person who keeps a first edition comic sealed in an airtight plastic bag and records notes on its history and value. This kind of passion and concern with detail drives most curators. Behind the baseball museum is someone who really loves the sport and all the stats. The craft museum is curated by someone who lives for handcrafted treasures.

Fueled by their passion, museum curators maintain and build collections for private citizens, nonprofit organizations, governments, businesses, associations, and colleges. Most organize art collections, but museums also house artifacts pertaining to natural history, American history, rock and roll, glass, fashion, or items you'd never guess. There are small museums devoted to shoes, the circus, comic strips, even nuts. (If you're ever in Sulabh, India, be sure to visit the International Museum of Toilets. Or how about the Burlingame Museum of Pez Memorabilia near San Francisco?) All told, there are some 5,000 museums in the United States and the mix almost certainly includes something to satisfy even the most eccentric tastes.

Get Started Now!

Put your museum career plans on display by
- Enjoying a rich, well-rounded education heavy with history and art appreciation courses.
- Volunteering or working part time at a museum. Many museums offer internships as well.
- Visiting as many museums as possible to develop an appreciation for the contributions curators and other museum staff make to each exhibit.

Hire Yourself!

You're curator at the Smithsonian's prestigious American History Museum (could be true someday!). The museum is planning a major new exhibit called "Turn of the 21st Century" which will showcase life in the United States at the beginning of the 2000s. Your job is to create a time capsule of sorts for an exhibit that realistically portrays what it was like to be a teenager at this point in history. The exhibit can focus on fashion, school life, favorite sports, favorite entertainers, and role models, or a mix of it all. Use drawings, photos, and pictures from magazines, catalogs, or websites to create a 3-D diorama that illustrates how the exhibit will look when complete. Also, include preliminary ideas for captions and narration so that museum visitors can get a better understanding of what the exhibit is all about.

As the experts, curators decide on themes for shows and how to best display works. They may arrange items chronologically or by similarities (e.g., jewel boxes all made of jade). They decide how pieces should be lit and choose the text that will best inform the museum visitor. They oversee the content for catalogs, guides, videos, and audiotapes about the exhibits.

At big museums, curators work with trained professionals to maintain and build a collection. Many pieces of art decay when exposed to air, certain types of light, and high temperatures, so curators rely on conservators for their expertise in preservation. When a piece does need a repair, the conservator takes care of restoring it. Humans are also a threat, so art is often kept under glass or behind laser-alarms that are triggered when curious or thieving hands come too close.

Museums can house thousands of items, and curators must have a record of each one. To keep track, the curator turns to the registrar, who keeps the paperwork on the history of all items. Often, curators arrange for photos to be taken to maintain as a reference if items are ever damaged or stolen.

Their voluminous knowledge is vital when purchasing new items for a museum. Scrutinizing pieces often with a magnifying glass, curators can verify a work's authenticity.

Writing skills are a must for curators. As new pieces come in, they must all be described and classified. Also, curators often publish articles in journals and magazines, and they may write the text for all literature pertaining to an exhibit. Curators need to be good public speakers as well, as they are occasionally called upon by the media to explain exhibits. Social savvy is key during fund-raising events and conducting tours for dignitaries and researchers. And some business knowledge comes in handy since many of the duties are administrative—handling budgets, hiring staff, and purchasing supplies. As more cataloging and record-keeping are done via computers and scanning, curators need to know a bit about technology as well.

At larger museums, you'll find these duties spread out among a highly specialized staff that may include

- An administrator who handles the business side of things and manages matters such as personnel, budget, and building maintenance
- An archivist who organizes important historical documents, photographs, films, and other important documents
- A conservator who examines, repairs, and restores art objects
- A registrar who acts as legal guardian for a museum and keeps records that indicate where every single item entrusted to the museum is located, where it came from, how it is insured, and how to take care of it

There is no denying that museum work is a highly competitive field. But those up for the challenge and equipped with generous doses of dedication and passion for a particular subject can expect to find interesting and fulfilling opportunities.

music composer

music composer Whether your taste in music runs to rap, rock, country, or pop, the music you listen to comes compliments of a composer. Composers write the music you hear on the radio, on CDs, in movies, and on television. When an orchestra hits a moving crescendo in a Beethoven symphony or a band rocks out to a tune by the Rolling Stones, a composer is the artist behind the sounds you hear.

No doubt about it, music carries tremendous power. It makes people dance and sing, it can soothe and calm jangled nerves, it can rouse patriotic sentiments, and stir virtually every emotion known to mankind. It can make you laugh, it can make you cry, and it can even frighten you out of your wits. Next time you watch a scary movie, think about how the background music intensifies your fear.

None of this happens by accident. Like all artists, composers rely on a unique mix of skill, talent, and inspiration to create original work. The best composers somehow manage to transform little squiggly notes on paper into musical masterpieces with the potential to transcend time itself. If you've ever heard Handel's *Messiah*, Beethoven's Fifth Symphony or just about anything by Rodgers and Hammerstein, you know exactly what we're talking about.

Composers craft a composition using the tools of music theory and notation. Because they understand the capabilities of instruments and voices, they enrich their compositions with solos, harmonies, rhythms,

Get Started Now!

As an overture to a career in composing, take these measures:

- Sign up for band, chorus, and other music courses offered at your school.
- Take music lessons, both for playing an instrument and music theory.

Search It!
The American Composers Alliance at ***www.composers.com*** and Recording Industry Association of America at ***www.riaa.com***

Read It!
Articles and resources at ***www.songwriting.com*** and ***www.lyricist.com***

Learn It!
Bachelor's or master's degree in music, music history, music performance, or music composition

Earn It!
Median annual salary is $31,310. (Source: U.S. Department of Labor)

Find It!
The "big five" in recording are BMG Entertainment at ***www.bmg.com***, Warner Brothers Music at ***www.wbr.com***, EMI Group at ***www.emigroup.com***, Sony Music Entertainment at ***www.sonymusic.com***, and Universal Music Group at ***www.umusic.com***.

Hire Yourself!

Imagine this. It's graduation day (hurray!), and because of your impeccable taste and good judgment, your school principal has put you in charge of selecting music for the ceremony. The traditional "Pomp and Circumstance" will make its expected appearances at the beginning and end of the program, but it's up to you to choose five songs that best reflect the common experiences your classmates have shared over the past four years. Which five songs fit the bill? The songs can be old, new, or a combination of the two. It's certainly okay to add an original composition of your own to the mix. Make a list, find copies of the lyrics on-line, and put all your ideas together in a nice folder to present to the graduation committee.

and melodies. Knowing how to read and play music is second nature for the composer, but getting to that point requires "practice, practice, practice," as the saying goes. By practicing the great pieces of music, those starting out can learn the basics of song construction. Famous composers from Mozart to Gershwin have all learned from the masters who went before them.

Some composers are also songwriters—the main difference being that composers write the music, while the songwriter writes the words or lyrics to a song.

Job opportunities are as diverse as the different types of composers in the world. However, each path takes a lot of dedication and initiative. Orchestras need new symphonies to play, but composing these pieces requires years of training, performing, and conducting. Writing pop songs might be easier, but you have to be resourceful to get songs recorded and played on radio stations or on MTV. Take a close listen around and you may be surprised how often you hear original tunes—on television, in movies, for advertisements, and even in video games. Although the field can be competitive, those lucky to have that creative spark and the drive to succeed should take heart, because the world will always need music.

musician From rappers to bagpipe players, musicians are an incredibly diverse group. No matter the type of musician (or singer), each has the unique ability to make sounds that move people—both emotionally and physically. Whether their instrument is guitar, harmonica, tuba, or even the human voice, musicians have mastered music fundamentals such as melody, harmony, and rhythm. Because they have years of practice invested in their art, musicians are comfortable playing in front of an audience. They are entertainers and they can't afford to be shy about getting on stage and expressing themselves.

Late schedules are the norm because most performances are at night and on weekends. To get from one gig to the next, some musicians become real road warriors, spending long stretches driving or in the air. When not performing live, they are often recording music in professional studios, making music for albums, movies, TV shows, and other media. Recording requires a lot of patience because sound engineers often demand multiple "takes" to get the recording exactly right.

The rest of their time is devoted to practice, practice, practice. That's the only way to stay proficient. Some musicians take lessons throughout their career to keep improving, and almost all have had classes in music

Get Started Now!

Want to make music? Start tuning up by doing the following:

- Take music classes in school. Study an instrument and join a school band or orchestra.
- Take advantage of opportunities to perform and compete. Battle of the Bands? Be there and do your best!
- Expand your musical repertoire by listening to all kinds of music and reading about both well-known and up-and-coming musicians.

Search It!
American Federation of Musicians at ***www.afm.org*** and American Guild of Musical Artists at ***www.musicialartists.com***

Read It!
International Musician magazine at ***www.afm.org***, Harmony Central website at ***harmony-central.com***, and the "future of music careers" at ***www.musicdish.com***

Learn It!
To find out about music programs, contact the National Association of Schools of Music at ***www.arts-accredit.org*** and MusicStaff.com at ***www.musicstaff.com/university***.

Earn It!
Median annual salary is $36,290. (Source: U.S. Department of Labor)

Find It!
Check out Jobs for Musicians at ***www.jobsformusicians.com***, Ultimatetalent.com at ***www.ultimatetalent.com***, and Busy Musician at ***www.busymusician.com***.

Hire Yourself!

Ready for prime time? A good rule of thumb is that you are ready to perform when you can proficiently play 40 songs all the way through. Make two lists. On the first list write the names of songs you already know. On the second, make a list of songs you'd really love to learn. Then, for the sake of this activity, assume that you'll be performing these songs at your band's first big gig. Use a software program like Microsoft Word or Publisher to create a snazzy musical program to pass out to your listeners. Divide the music into four sets of 10 songs, paying particular attention to grouping songs in an especially appealing and entertaining way.

theory, composition, and instrumental instruction. To play pieces of music alone and with others, they have to know how to read sheet music.

Getting gigs can mean auditioning or leaving behind demo tapes that show a performer's talent at its best. As with actors, many musicians depend on agents to handle their careers, negotiate contracts, and find them work. Agents are always looking for opportunities—operas, musical comedies, ballets, marching bands, weddings—any productions that pay their musicians. Most have to like city living because most jobs are in major metropolitan areas. Until they have steady work in music, musicians hold other part-time jobs to support themselves. The Bureau of Labor Statistics says that three-quarters of musicians perform part-time.

Work conditions depend on the type of production involved. Whereas rock bands may work in smoky clubs or outdoor amphitheaters, classical musicians usually perform in concert halls. This is a very competitive field so those interested in music often pursue related occupations, such as composer, music therapist, music teacher, concert manager, music store owner, music critic, or instrument repairer.

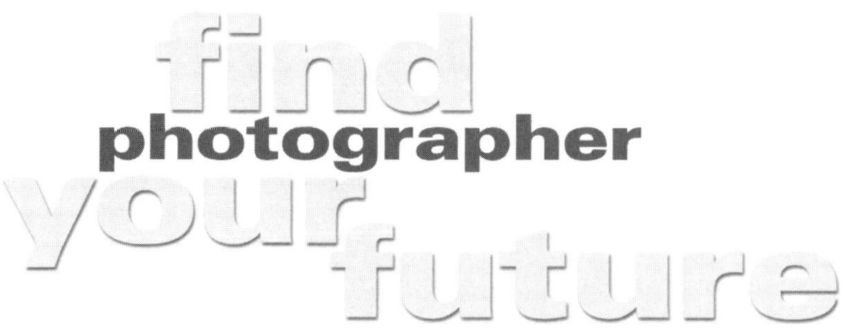

photographer You could say that photographers live for the moment—that precise moment in time when the lighting is just right, the action memorable, and the subject expressive. If they do their job correctly, they capture that moment on film. To do this, photographers need an artistic eye, an almost uncanny sense of observation, impeccable timing, and a very friendly relationship with a very important piece of equipment—their camera.

Photographers' cameras are their livelihood—along with accessories such as tripods and lighting. Photographers have complete knowledge of their cameras' apertures, lenses, and overall capabilities. To get their subjects looking natural and attractive, photographers must master people skills as well. They have to build a quick rapport with their subjects to help them relax and draw out different expressions and emotions.

Of all the types of photographers, photojournalist may be the first that comes to mind. Following assignments from magazine and newspaper editors, these professionals record news-making events, shooting at crime scenes, on battlefields, outside courtrooms, or at the White House. They may photograph basketball games and mountain climbing or wait patiently to capture a candid shot of a celebrity.

Get Started Now!

Here's how to develop a career in photography:

- Volunteer as staff photographer for your school newspaper or yearbook.
- Take photography classes offered through your school, your community's continuing education programs, or a local photography store.
- Become a shutterbug. Take photos at sporting events, family gatherings, and on vacations.

Search It!
Professional Photographers of America at ***www.ppa.com***, the Association of Photographers at ***www.the-aop.org***, and American Society of Media Photographers at ***www.asmp.org***

Read It!
Profotos on-line photography magazine at ***www.profotos.com/education/promag/index.shtml*** and AOP's Career Advice at ***www.the-aop.org/home.htm***

Learn It!
- No requirements other than talent and experience, but technical training or a degree can help
- Some high-level positions at major newspapers or magazines require a bachelor's or master's degree

Earn It!
Median annual salary is $24,040. (Source: U.S. Department of Labor)

Find It!
Visit *National Geographic* at ***www.nationalgeographic.com*** and *TravelAmerica* at ***www.travelamerica.com***.

Hire Yourself!

The local chamber of commerce just hired you to create a vacation guide designed to lure visitors to your hometown. Your job is to capture on film the town's top 10 hotspots. Use the best camera you can (even if it's one of those handy dandy disposable cameras you can get from the grocery store) and hit the road. Plan each shot carefully, testing various angles to get just the right look. Make sure to get a good mix of shots including landscapes, buildings, and people. Have the film developed and attach your best shots to poster board to create an enticing montage.

Commercial photographers stage indoor and outdoor photo shoots that meet specific client needs. An ad agency for a soup company may want the perfect photo of a steamy bowl of chowder for a new campaign. A dog magazine may want a cover with three prize-winning pooches posing against a white backdrop. Some photographers strictly focus on fashion, taking shots of models for magazines and designers.

Every community also has its share of wedding and portrait photographers who capture some of life's most memorable moments on film. On the cutting edge in photography are scientific and medical photographers. Medical photographers shoot surgeries and other treatments to record for future reference and research. Some specialize in photomicrography, or photographing microscopic objects so they appear in full detail.

To get into the career, many begin as assistants to professional photographers, where they can learn many of the technical aspects, including how to develop film, mix chemicals, and make prints. It pays to be physically fit, too. Photographers are always lugging around equipment, and they frequently travel and move with the action to capture ideal moments.

Those dedicated to the career keep up with technological advances: today's digital photography is changing the way photos are taken and printed. Because most earn money as freelancers, basic business knowledge can help. Photography is one of those professions where equal parts of talent, creativity, and persistence—and a great camera, of course—can come together with some very exciting opportunities.

printer When you first think of a career in printing, you may think it's just about producing magazines, newspapers, and books. But take a closer look around your world, and you'll find printing on cereal boxes, menus, CD covers, billboards, and more. Anywhere ink is on paper, a printer has been at work.

Printing is one of the oldest professions. It started in Germany in 1400 with Johannes Gutenberg's first mechanical press. Ben Franklin and Mark Twain both worked as printers. Today, it is the third largest manufacturing industry in the country, according to the Graphic Arts Information Network.

The current process for mass-producing words and images on paper is highly technological. Printing presses are computerized (unlike the old days) and run in clean environments—rarely do you see a printing machine operator covered in ink as pages come off the press. Printers learn different skills depending on the print process. The dominant printing method is offset lithography. Lithographers transfer an inked impression from a rubber-covered cylinder to paper or other material. Other types of plate presses are gravure, flexography, screenprinting, and letterpress. Plateless processes, such as ink-jetting, are newer but growing.

Operating multimillion-dollar presses requires a unique combination of computer, math, science, mechanical, and electrical skills. Operators adjust printing plates, regulate ink pressure, and set paper sizes to be

Get Started Now!

Stop the presses! Here's how to get a career as a printer rolling:

- Look into apprenticeship programs through trade schools.
- Take an entry-level job with a major printing or publishing firm.
- Volunteer to handle the production side of printing your school newspaper or yearbook.

Search It!
National Association of Printers and Lithographers at ***www.napl.org*** and National Association for Printing Ink Manufacturers at ***www.napim.org***

Read It!
Printing Manager magazine at ***www.napl.org/publications/printing_manager.htm*** and *PrintAction* at ***www.printaction.com***

Learn It!

- Technical training in printing or printing technology suggested
- Accredited training programs listed at ***www.npes.org/gaerf/PrintED/accredschools.html***
- On-the-job training and apprenticeships

Earn It!
Median annual salary is $29,010. (Source: U.S. Department of Labor)

Find It!
Printing companies include Quebecor at ***www.quebecor.com*** and Worldcolor at ***www.worldcolor.net***.

Hire Yourself!

How does the printing process work? Go to the How Stuff Works website at ***http://entertainment.howstuffworks.com/offset-printing.htm*** to find out. Use the information you discover to create a printing timeline that provides a step-by-step description of the printing process from beginning to end.

printed. They closely monitor the ink distribution and colors, and they closely analyze printed test sheets to make sure the product is meeting all the client's specifications. If a magazine is being printed, a production manager from the publication will work with the printer to assure that the job is printed correctly. Taking direction from the production manager, the printer may have to lighten the red on the cover or increase the black on the body type.

Printers must keep a close eye on the process because if anything is being printed incorrectly, the cost in wasted paper and ink can skyrocket. Their mechanical talents come in especially handy when there is an equipment malfunction. It's a very active, physical job, loading paper and ink and pulling printed product off the presses. Hours are often long to meet client deadlines.

Nowadays, printed material originates as files on computers. Before printing begins, a prepress expert prepares computer files, relying on specialized computer knowledge. The prepress person knows how to adjust type, images, and color within a computer file. At the end of the printing process, manufacturing specialists are needed to handle cutting, collating, and binding material.

Opportunities for printers should grow as the demand for books and magazines continues to increase, especially in foreign markets. Also, as long as marketers keep sending direct mail pieces to stuff our mailboxes, printing will remain a booming industry.

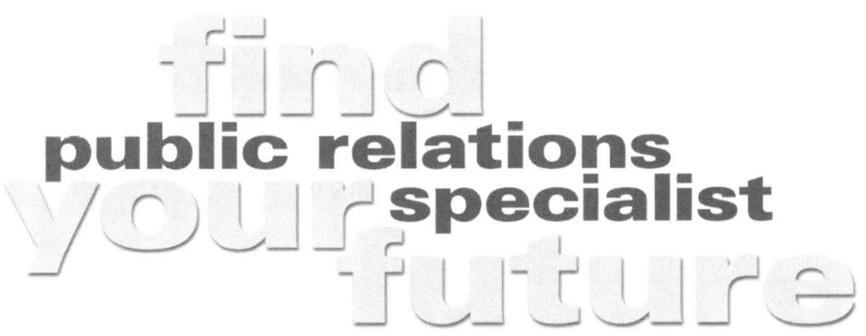

public relations specialist

Newsflash! A major organization needs to get an important message out to the general public. Who is it going to call? This is a job for a public relations specialist. Also called public information officers, these professionals work for organizations to make the public aware of their new programs, policies, and achievements.

If Coke is adding lemon to its soda or if Toyota is introducing a new car for Millennials (that's what marketing experts call people in your generation), PR specialists spring into action. They determine what media sources are most likely to be receptive to the news and create a media action plan. Then they write press releases explaining why this story is of interest, making it as compelling as possible because so many different stories are competing for media attention. Many news stories originate from the desks of PR specialists, and if journalists have questions or seek other information about an organization, they turn to the PR specialist for answers.

When the public likes your company, they tend to buy more of your product. So a lot of this job is about maintaining a favorable public image.

Get Started Now!

Can you relate to the public? Find out if this career for you.

- Take all the courses you can in written and verbal communication including speech, debate, composition, and creative writing.
- Get involved in the school paper or yearbook.
- Check into internship opportunities at pubic relations firms and the communications departments of major corporations.

Search It!
Public Relations Society of America at ***www.prsa.org***; the Institute for PR, ***www.instituteforpr.com***; and International Association of Business Communicators, ***www.iabc.com***.

Read It!
PR Matters newsletter at ***www.learnpr.com/current_newsletter.htm*** and *PRWeek* at ***www.prweekus.com***

Learn It!
Bachelor's degree in public relations, communications, journalism, or advertising

Earn It!
Median annual salary is $41,710. (Source: U.S. Department of Labor)

Find It!
Corporations, nonprofit organizations, and the government need public relations specialists. Visit Weber Shandwick at ***www.webershandwick.com***, Publicis at ***www.publicis.com***, and Fleishman-Hillard at ***www.fleishman.com***.

Hire Yourself!

Spread the word. Your high school just won an award for best all-around high school in the county. Use information you find at ***www.press-release-writing.com*** to write an official press release that outlines at least five programs, teachers, and other reasons that make your school a cut above the rest. Use an attention-getting headline and proper formatting so that media professionals take your press release seriously.

Sometimes, however, bad news strikes and the PR specialist's skills get put to the test. This is when it helps to possess a great presence of mind, sensitivity, and sharp communication skills in addressing the public.

Think of how hard the job is for the PR person working for a petroleum company that has just had a major oil spill. Sarah Jones, president of the Canadian Public Relations Society, once commented that in a negative publicity scenario you "take immediate action, you worry about the people first, you provide as much information as possible as fast as you've got it."

Even when there is no news, PR directors are always thinking of clever ways to gain positive media attention for their company. It takes a creative mind to come up with gimmicks like the Good Year blimp or Oscar Mayer's Weinermobile, both of which have been turning heads for decades. To gain publicity during the splashdown of the Soviet Mir Space station, the communications team at Taco Bell came up with an inspired idea. The company created a 40 x 40-foot vinyl target displaying its logo and the words "Free Taco Here." Taco Bell floated the target in the ocean off of Australia and promised to give free tacos to everyone in America if the shuttle hit the bulls-eye. A minute-by-minute countdown of the descent was broadcast on the Internet and the Taco Bell target was seen by millions of Web surfers.

To be successful at this career, you need strong communication and organizational skills, sociability, and creativity. While PR professionals write and edit press releases, annual reports, newsletters, and brochures, they also organize meetings, press conferences, and interviews. They set up speaking appearances for corporate officials and write their speeches.

If you're interested in communications, this may be a good time to pursue a PR career. A recent report from the Council of Public Relations Firms shows that business is booming for major PR firms, which translates into opportunities for up-and-coming PR professionals.

publisher When the Internet became such a huge phenomenon, people predicted the death of the printed word and the end to many traditional careers in publishing. But the predictions were wrong. In fact, the niche magazine business is on the rise, and book sales have been inching up in recent years (maybe a young man named Harry Potter or Oprah's Book Club are to be thanked). Opportunities in publishing may be more susceptible than some to swings in the economy, but the industry as a whole is still thriving.

Traditionally, publishers are the chief operating officers of the print industry. With their keen business management skills, they serve as the guiding light behind every book, magazine, and newspaper. The field is so varied it includes everything from medical publications to children's books and even phone directories. Think of a topic and there's probably something being published about it.

To sell the printed word, publishers coordinate several components—editorial, sales, circulation, and production. The engine that sustains any successful publishing firm is content, because ultimately that is what people are buying. If your content is serving your audience, they will

Get Started Now!

Want to work in the whirlwind world of words? Explore publishing by doing the following:

- High school course schedules should include as many literature courses as possible, as well as any business and leadership courses you can squeeze in.
- Read, read, read—the classics, the current bestsellers, the newspaper. Devour anything that gives you an idea of the kinds of work that publishers publish.
- Involvement in the school newspaper, yearbook, and any other project that hones communication skills is encouraged.

Search It!
Editor & Publisher at ***www.editorandpublisher.com***, Small Publishers Association of North America (SPAN) at ***www.spannet.org***, Association of Educational Publishers at ***www.edpress.org***, and Association of American Publishers at ***www.publishers.org***

Read It!
Publishers Weekly at ***www.publishersweekly.reviewsnews.com***

Learn It!
- Bachelor's degree in public relations, communications, journalism, or advertising
- Master's degree in business administration is helpful

Earn It!
Salaries vary widely according to the size of the operation.

Find It!
Check out Scholastic Inc. at ***www.scholastic.com*** and Condé Nast at ***www.condenet.com/condenast***.

Hire Yourself!

They're finally listening! The local school board has decided to offer a course in contemporary literature that high school students actually want to read. Your job is to come up with a list of the top 10 favorite teen novels and download information about them from websites such as ***www.amazon.com***, ***www.bn.com***, and ***www.borders.com***. Use the information you find to create a minicatalog that teachers and other schools might use to order the books.

keep coming back for more. Golf magazines must provide the latest techniques and golf news to those devoted to the links. Medical publications have to report on the newest advances for health care professionals. A publisher relies on a strong editor to assure content is meeting the needs of the audience. The overall design of a publication is almost as important as the content because a reader will not pick up a book, magazine, or newspaper if it doesn't look appealing.

Perhaps the biggest question to answer is: Where is the money coming from? Some publications, like books and certain magazines, rely strictly on sales to the customer. Magazines and newspapers depend on subscriptions, newsstand sales, and, most of all, advertising. A top team of advertising representatives and marketers are needed to sell ad space. Magazine publishers often must analyze the market carefully to be sure there are enough companies who want to advertise their product to the specific audience and that there is not too much competition from other magazines.

With content and funding in place, how will the materials reach the audience? To carry out this function, publishers depend on a circulation (or distribution) department. Free weekly newspapers, for example, are often distributed through street boxes and at the entrances to different shops.

To assure the quality and cost of their product, publishers devote time to getting the best manufacturing and printing for the money. Often working with a production manager, publishers make printing decisions regarding paper weight, binding, and color reproduction.

In many cases, publishers come from a background in sales and marketing. They are constantly concerned with the budget and operating expenses. To grow the company, they cultivate strategic partnerships and come up with related products or new publications. To save money, many publishers outsource services, hiring freelance editors and designers, for example. Those who advance keep abreast of industry trends, such as ways to publish and make money on the Web.

scriptwriter "You want the truth. You can't handle the truth!" Jack Nicholson may have immortalized those words in the movie *A Few Good Men*, but it was the scriptwriter Aaron Sorkin who really deserves the credit. Every word of dialogue you hear uttered on television or at the movies originated in the mind of the scriptwriter. Directors and actors may get most of the attention in the entertainment industry, but the scriptwriter's original stories are the backbone of the industry.

Film and television careers are glamorous and exciting, but they are very difficult fields to break into. Making it takes talent, networking, and endless hard work. First and foremost, scriptwriters are amazing wordsmiths. They've had plenty of experience writing, and they have many ideas for original stories. Those with a strong background in literature and English are often good at coming up with plot lines and vivid characters. Professionals who represent scriptwriters are even called literary agents.

A script will never be read unless it is properly formatted according to industry standards. Formatting helps directors and technicians plan the schedule for shooting each scene. Producers and agents find it easier to review scripts that adhere to the established style. Following the format,

Get Started Now!

Start rolling in a career as scriptwriter:

- Read as many scripts as possible. You can download them for free at ***www.scriptcrawler.com***, ***www.iscriptdb.com***, and ***www.simplyscript.com***.
- Watch movies with an ear for dialogue, an eye for action, and a mind for plot development. Outline the plots of your favorite films to get a sense of their structure.
- If you're really motivated, check out screenwriting contests by searching on-line.

Search It!
American Screenwriter's Association at ***www.asascreenwriters.com***

Read It!
Hollywood Scriptwriter at ***www.hollywoodscriptwriter.com*** and *Scriptwriter* magazine at ***www.scriptwritermagazine.com***

Learn It!

- Postsecondary degree in film or writing recommended to develop the craft and make vital industry contacts
- Intern on a movie set or at a literary agency that handles screenwriters

Earn It!
Median annual salary is $42,790. (writers and authors)
(Source: U.S. Department of Labor)

Find It!
Check out film studios, television networks, and cable television stations, such as New Line Cinema at ***www.newline.com***, Fox at ***www.fox.com***, and HBO at ***www.hbo.com***.

Hire Yourself!

A public television station is looking for short films about issues relevant to today's teens to run after programming that isn't quite an hour long. Write an original short script that could be easily filmed and runs about 10 minutes. To make the script more authentic, download and use free scriptwriting software at ***www.scriptbuddy.com*** or ***www.storymind.com*** to use in formatting your script.

Remember, all good writing is rewriting, so work out the kinks to get your script ready for prime time!

scriptwriters know exactly how many pages to write for specific lengths of time—a TV sitcom will be much shorter than a feature film.

With practice, screenwriters develop the language needed to create dialogue, action, and plot lines. Once that skill is mastered, those starting out need to make industry connections. That sometimes means moving to New York City or Los Angeles. Then, writers need an agent who can sell the work to film and television producers. Getting an agent is a job in itself, and you have to draw on all your social skills to meet agents and sell yourself. Selling your script idea means having your pitch down—you must be able to get people excited about it.

It's a bit of a catch-22, but having a script already produced can help you break into the business. For a beginner, this may mean working with an independent or student filmmaker. Many successful screenwriters start by writing independent features, some that they fund and direct themselves. Before getting the chance to sell a full script, many professionals are asked to write scripts on speculation or "spec." These aren't always full scripts but detailed outlines. Studios and production companies review spec scripts but they don't pay a dime unless they decide to buy. Keep in mind, too, that some scripts are bought but not necessarily made—they wind up gathering dust in the studio vaults and never make it to the screen.

Those who succeed in this career are usually thick-skinned; they can withstand a lot of rejection on the road to finally selling a script. They are also not married to their work because scripts are often rewritten or doctored by others. Besides hustling to sell work to major motion picture studios and television shows, writers can find opportunities with educational videos, documentaries, commercials, and cartoons.

set and exhibit designer

Set and exhibit designers have the amazing ability to create—or re-create—entire worlds. In the movies, when you see a diner or mission control at NASA, these are often environments reimagined by a set designer. Some films construct new places entirely from the designer's imagination, such as the school for wizards in *Harry Potter* or space stations depicted in *Star Wars*. In theaters, too, settings come alive—whether it is a nightclub in the musical *Cabaret* or a Chinese palace in the opera *Turandot*.

Perhaps one of the most famous Broadway sets was for *Miss Saigon*, which, in one scene, re-created a realistic hovering helicopter. If the set designer has done his or her job properly, the audience does not even question the reality of what they are seeing.

As key players on the teams that produce theater, film, and television, set designers consult closely with writers and directors to form an artistic vision for the surroundings in which the actors will perform. A background in art and drawing certainly helps when it comes to sketching out concepts. But today's sophisticated software lets designers visualize on a computer monitor. With computer-aided design (CAD), changes are a snap. Want to add in a staircase or subtract red curtains? Simply type the instructions on the keyboard and enter. In fact, some film sets exist entirely on a computer's hard drive.

Get Started Now!

Set yourself up to be a star designer:

- Volunteer to help build the set of a community or school play.
- Lend a hand getting together the props on a low-budget movie.

Search It!
AssistantDirectors.com at ***http://assistantdirectors.com***

Read It!
Find links to all kinds of theater resources at ***www.artslynx.org***.

Learn It!

- Bachelor's degree in theater arts, technical theater, or set design
- Visit the website for the National Association of Schools of Art and Design at ***http://nasad.arts-accredit.org/index.jsp.***

Earn It!
Median annual salary is $33,870. (Source: U.S. Department of Labor)

Find It!
Explore Universal Pictures at ***www.universalpictures.com*** and Vancouver Film Studios at ***www.vancouverfilmstudios.com***. Check out the Smithsonian at ***www.si.edu,*** the Exploris at ***www.exploris.org***, and ***www.seaworld.com.***

Hire Yourself!

Choose three television shows—a sitcom, a national news show (morning or evening), and a made-for-TV movie. Watch each show (mute the sound if you want to cut down on distractions) and take detailed notes of the various sets used throughout each show. After you've watched all these shows, prepare a chart describing each show, comparing the similarities and differences. Summarize your opinion about how well the sets enhanced each show by assigning a letter grade from A to F.

Still, most sets rise from the hard work of a construction team. All professionals at some point get their hands dirty painting backdrops, sawing wood, and rigging wires. Designers coordinate lights to change the dramatic mood. Some work with engineers building elaborate hydraulics that lift and lower scenery. Often they turn to a prop manager, who may have to comb flea markets and secondhand shops to find the right period pieces of furniture.

Top designers must be keen managers as well—they follow budgets, set schedules, order supplies, direct workers, and make sure all components are in place to complete the project on time. Because of budget constraints, designers often must be masters of illusion who can make do with less—manipulating low-cost elements to produce high-quality visuals.

Museums and galleries provide equally exciting and challenging venues for a similar type of design expertise. Additional opportunities for set designers are found in the commercial world in places such as restaurants, shopping malls, and trade shows. TV commercials, museums and galleries—all of these require planning to create ambience, showcase work, and provide interactive educational exhibits.

Here's a news flash likely to impact up-and-coming set designers: think virtual. As technology continues to dazzle us with increased capabilities, it's quite likely that the new breed of set designers will increasingly trade in their hammers for a computer mouse to create sets for news programs, television game shows, commercials, and feature-length films.

technical writer

technical writer If you've ever read the instructions on how to set up a stereo or program a VCR, you've seen the work of the technical writer. Technical writers translate scientific and technical information so the average person can understand it. But their job can be much more than writing instructions for household gizmos. They also write computer software manuals, catalogs, parts lists, marketing materials, project proposals, web pages, lab reports, newsletters, and employee handbooks and training manuals. The level of writing complexity depends on who the audience is and the purpose of the project. A guide on software for nuclear research technicians will be more complex than the operating instructions for an electric can opener.

No matter what the job, technical writers are experts at giving directions. They use words to teach others how to do things. Simplifying complicated processes into terms anyone can understand takes more than a little research. In fact, seasoned technical writers estimate that the

Get Started Now!

Here are instructions on how to explore a career in technical writing:

- Stack your schedule with composition and creative writing courses.
- Make sure you know your way around a computer and the Internet—tools of choice for technical writers everywhere.
- Develop your writing skills whenever possible by volunteering for the school newspaper and yearbook and helping out with the weekly bulletin at your favorite place of worship.

Search It!
Society for Technical Communications at ***htpp://stc.org*** and TECHW-RL at ***www.raycomm.com/techwhirl***

Read It!
Technical Communication magazine at ***www.techcomm-online.org*** and TECHW-RL on-line magazine at ***www.raycomm.com/techwhirl/magazine/index.html***

Learn It!

- Degree from a two-year or four-year college in technical communications
- Browse technical communication programs at ***htpp://stc.org/academic_database.asp***
- Bachelor's degree in English, journalism, or communications

Earn It!
Median annual salary is $50,580. (Source: U.S. Department of Labor)

Find It!
Visit NASA at ***www.nasa.gov***, Wolfram Research at ***www.wolfram.com***, and Microsoft at ***www.microsoft.com***.

Hire Yourself!

Write an Operator's Manual for your home. You and your family are going on a vacation and a dependable friend is going to mind the house. Your job is to write instructions so that your family's plants, pets, and possessions are still alive and well upon your return.

How do the VCR, stereo, and computer work? What are the directions for feeding any pets and tending to any plants? When should garbage be taken out? Where should mail be stored? Put it all together in a well-organized folder or notebook.

job is really 70 percent research and 30 percent writing. Only by spending time with a product, using it extensively, and taking notes on its operation, can you properly explain how it works. Because they gain an in-depth knowledge of certain products and systems, tech writers often become specialists in certain fields, such as agriculture, pharmaceuticals, and telecommunications.

Organized, methodical thinking is key to this job. You can't miss a step or be out of order with directions or the results could be disastrous—think how important accurate writing would be in a manual on how to fly and land a plane. Although hours are spent alone researching and writing, technical writers may collaborate with an art director and freelance writers to put together a project. They also interview experts and typically translate their knowledge into simpler terms—brilliant scientists and researchers may know all about nuclear fusion and fluid dynamics, but they may not be able to tell a paragraph from a paramecium.

Because many tech writers are freelancers, they depend on industry contacts and a portfolio full of previous writing to win new assignments. Although it can be stressful churning out writing on deadline, these professionals find rewards in constantly discovering how things work.

webmaster Britney Spears has one. *The Simpsons* has one. The U.S. Government has lots of them. Just about every company in America has one nowadays. We're talking about a website—an efficient way to provide information and communications through computers. Just go on-line using a computer at home, school, or the library, and you will discover an endless number of websites.

How did all this great information get out there? Thank the webmaster—a new profession, unheard of when your parents were your age, that has sprung up with the growth of the Internet.

When it comes to creating a website, many different skills come into play—and the successful webmaster is, naturally, master of them all. He or she understands how the entire process works—from the beginning stages of coming up with an idea for a site to ultimately launching it online and keeping it up-to-date.

A great website starts with content. A web surfer will click off a site in seconds if there's nothing there of substance or if it's not organized in a friendly way. The webmaster helps define the purpose of the site and determines the kinds of information typical users will want to find. Collaborating with clients can be the key to the content. A bookstore, for example, may want a site to tout the latest bestsellers, announce spe-

Get Started Now!

Click on to a career as webmaster:

- Sign up for basic computer training courses, graphic design courses, and computer programming (especially any that focus on HTML language) at your school or community continuing education system.
- Learn to find your way around the Internet by using it to research homework assignments and stay in touch with friends and family.

Search It!
World Organization of Webmasters at ***www.joinwow.org*** and Webmasters Marketing Association at ***www.webmasters.org***

Read It!
Web Developer's Journal at ***www.webdevelopersjournal.com***; WebProfession, ***www.webprofession.com***; and the Web Developer's Virtual Library at ***www.wdvl.com***

Learn It!

- Technical schools and community colleges generally have two-year training programs
- Browse training programs at ***www.iwanet.org/training/atsearch.html***
- Training as a graphic designer

Earn It!
Median annual salary is $58,420. (Source: U.S. Department of Labor)

Find It!
Check out POP Interactive at ***www.popinteractive.com*** and Out of Web Site at ***www.outofwebsite.com***.

Hire Yourself!

The good, the bad, the ugly. You be the judge when it comes to picking the best and worst websites. Your job is to find five exceptional websites and five truly awful ones.

For good ones use your personal favorites or look for award-winners at websites like *Time*'s 50 Best Websites at ***www.time.com/time/2002/tech/best***; Web 100, with lists updated by the hour at ***www.web100.com***; and the Best Websites Directory at ***www.bestwebsites.com.my***.

For bad ones, add websites you've found on your own with the worst of the worst (in your opinion) found at websites like Useless Pages at ***www.go2net.com/useless*** and Web Pages That Suck at ***http://webpagesthatsuck.com***.

Create a poster display of your findings. Make sure to include five elements common to good websites and five mistakes commonly found at bad ones.

cial events and sales, and provide a way to take credit card orders. A major decision can be picking the name of the site or the URL address.

With purpose and content set, the webmaster needs to think of how to make everything look attractive. What photos and art will wow the web user? A webmaster may direct a graphic designer to concoct eye-catching pages, incorporating logos, icons, buttons, colors, type faces, side bars, and menus. Graphic design requires computer know-how of Photoshop software, jpeg compression, scanners, and more.

With content and visuals in mind, a web architect plans the flow of the site. Where will users click? How will they navigate through? What pages and images will users go through to get to the information they need? The architect may work with a web technician to execute the plan.

The web technician changes content into documents that you can see on your computer screen using something called HTML (hypertext markup language). Good computer code is the foundation of a website. Technicians bring animation and sound to websites by coding in programs such as Real Audio and Shockwave.

Once every element is ready, the site is launched and maintained on a web server. A website administrator may take care of these issues—plus they troubleshoot and provide security for web server hardware and software.

The webmaster can handle all the roles mentioned above or direct a staff that takes care of some of these duties. And don't think that this is just a job for computer nerds. Webmasters represent a cutting-edge career that demands creativity and keen people skills. Graphic design and basic Internet training are essential. Considering this career didn't even exist just 10 years ago, opportunities for webmasters look promising for the future. Websites have become as essential to doing business as the business card. Driven by the power of the Internet, websites are increasingly used to provide even the smallest business with worldwide audiences. Webmasters pave the way for this new global highway.

Search It!
Writers Guild of America at ***www.wga.org***, Writer's Resource Links at ***www.carolkluz.homestead.com/index1.html***, and ***bellaonline.com/articles/art2583.asp***

Read It!
Written By: The Magazine of the Writers Guild of America at ***www.wga.org/WrittenBy*** and Writer's Workshop at ***www.english.uiuc.edu/cws/wworkshop***

Learn It!
Degree in English, communications, or journalism

Earn It!
Median annual salary is $42,790 (Source: U.S. Department of Labor)

Find It!
Writers find opportunities with a diverse range of companies. Novelists can get a sense of the book publishing industry by visiting *Publisher's Weekly* on-line at ***www.publishersweekly.com***.

writer Although there are many different types of writers (see scriptwriter, page 101; journalist, page 80; technical writer, page 105), novelists are what most people think of when they hear the word "writer." Charles Dickens, Leo Tolstoy, and Ernest Hemingway are all famous authors whose works of literature we know from school courses. Many writers strive to produce classic works of literature that will be remembered throughout time.

The old saying goes that everyone has at least one good novel inside him or her, but to extract that novel takes incredibly hard work, focus, and imagination. First and foremost, writers have a way with words and love the writing process. You can become a better writer by practicing and taking courses, but that desire to churn out fiction comes from something internal—a burning need to express an idea or story. Novelists are also sharp observers of the human animal—they have an ear for dialogue and an eye for details. They often do research to make sure their work is historically accurate.

Writing novels is not a staff position, so professionals begin by squeezing in time to write while holding a day job. Wallace Stevens wrote while he was the vice president of an insurance company. T.S.

Get Started Now!

Commit yourself in ink to a career as a writer:

- Read as many books as possible. That will help you develop a love for books and appreciation of what goes into writing a novel.
- Keep a journal. By writing about your life on a daily basis you develop your skill as a writer.
- Take creative writing courses in high school, summer writing camps for teens (visit ***http://petersons.com/summerop*** for ideas), and your community continuing education system.

Hire Yourself!

Surely, you have a favorite author. Use the library and Internet resources to find out all you can about their work, their motivations, and their style. Use these discoveries to write a fictionalized account (at least 250 words) about a chance meeting between this author and an aspiring writer like you.

Eliot wrote while working as a banker, and William Carlos Williams composed and still kept to his duties as a doctor.

Sticking to a set schedule usually helps a writer complete the project. Authors need to set aside a specific time each day to write. They also need a space where they can think and focus on their composition. The tools of the trade are simple—a computer (although some very successful writers swear by the old-fashioned pad and pencil), a dictionary, thesaurus, and grammar guide.

To start the process, authors often make an outline of the story, describing the characters and setting and basic plot from start to finish. Novels have many parts, so some writers put their story ideas on index cards, so they can easily move around sections and figure out how the story should unfold. Vladimir Nabakov reportedly composed all his novels on index cards.

As if producing an entire book isn't hard enough, novelists have to be able to sell their work as well. Because most publishers do not review unsolicited manuscripts, writers sometimes sell to literary agents first, who in turn sell to the publishers. Advice for the young author: Never pay money to agents—they get paid by commission when they sell a book. To convince an agent to take them on, new authors need to have a completed manuscript. Pitching an agent begins with a query letter that sums up the book for the agent—providing the title, plot synopsis, and a sample of the writing. Most authors at some point must suffer through rejection and then buck up and send out their work again.

To get a break, writers attend conferences to network with agents and other authors. They also submit to writing contests, but primarily they continue to burn the midnight oil—writing late into the night and sending out letters to agents.

Big Question #5: do you have the right skills?

Career exploration is, in one sense, career matchmaking. The goal is to match your basic traits, interests and strengths, work values, and work personality with viable career options.

But the "stuff" you bring to a job is only half of the story.

Choosing an ideal job and landing your dream job is a two-way street. Potential employers look for candidates with specific types of skills and backgrounds. This is especially true in our technology-infused, global economy.

In order to find the perfect fit, you need to be fully aware of not only what you've got, but also what prospective employers need.

The following activity is designed to help you accomplish just that. This time we'll use the "wannabe" approach —working with careers you think you want to consider. This same matchmaking process will come in handy when it comes time for the real thing too.

Unfortunately, this isn't one of those "please turn to the end of the chapter and you'll find all the answers" types of activities. This one requires the best critical thinking, problem-solving, and decision-making skills you can muster.

Big Activity #5:
do you have the right skills?

Here's how it works:

Step 1: First, make a chart like the one on page 114.

Step 2: Next, pick a career profile that interests you and use the following resources to compile a list of the traits and skills needed to be successful. Include:

- Information featured in the career profile in this book;
- Information you discover when you look through websites of any of the professional associations or other resources listed with each career profile;
- Information from the career profiles and skills lists found on-line at America's Career InfoNet at ***www.acinet.org***.

Briefly list the traits or skills you find on separate lines in the first column of your chart.

Step 3: Evaluate yourself as honestly as possible. If, after careful consideration, you conclude that you already possess one of the traits or skills included on your list, place an *X* in the column marked "Got It!" If you conclude that the skill or trait is one you've yet to acquire, follow these directions to complete the column marked "Get It!":

- If you believe that gaining proficiency in a skill is just a matter of time and experience and you're willing to do whatever it takes to acquire that skill, place a *Y* (for yes) in the corresponding space.
- Or, if you are quite certain that a particular skill is one that you don't possess now, and either can't or won't do what it takes to acquire it, mark the corresponding space with an *N* (for no). For example, you want to be a brain surgeon. It's important, prestigious work and the pay is good. But, truth be told, you'd rather have brain surgery yourself than sit through eight more years of really intense science and math. This rather significant factor may or may not affect your ultimate career choice. But it's better to think it through now rather than six years into med school.

Step 4: Place your completed chart in your Big Question AnswerBook.

When you work through this process carefully, you should get some eye-opening insights into the kinds of careers that are right for you. Half reality check and half wake-up call, this activity lets you see how you measure up against important workforce competencies.

Big Activity #5: **do you have the right skills?**

skill or trait required	got it!	get it!

more career ideas in the arts and communications

There are a lot of career options in this book, but many more exist. Here is a list of a wide variety of additional professions for you to consider. If you think your future may lie in the arts and communications, use these ideas as a springboard for conducting ongoing research. Once you've had a chance to take a good look at the options, use the instructions included in Big Activity #6 to dig for more information.

The careers profiles featured in the previous section represent mainstream, highly viable occupations where someone with the right set of skills and training stands a good chance of starting a career. However, when it comes to careers in the arts, entertainment, and communications these careers are just the beginning. There are actually hundreds of possibilities for blending your passions and your abilities into a profession.

Some careers require top-notch talent, others a genuine interest in a certain aspect of the field (rock concert promoter, for example). Some are unusual, some obscure. For some you can walk into an employment agency to find a list of potential employers, for others, you have to carve out a little business niche of your own.

To keep things simple, each job title appears on only one list, the one that we believe represents the most predominant work personality type. However, as you've already learned, most jobs—and all people—are really unique combinations of more than one. Use your imagination here and look at these ideas as a way to get your creative juices flowing.

Accompanist
Advertisement Designer
Advertising Copywriter
Advertising Executive
Animal Trainer
Apparel Engineer
Archivist

Art Appraiser
Art Curriculum Writer
Art Festival Coordinator
Art Historian
Art Librarian
Art Registrar
Art Teacher

Artist Agent
Artist Manager
Arts Commission Liaison (at city or state government levels)
Arts Marketer
Auctioneer
Author
Automobile Designer
Ballet Dancer
Basket Maker
Best Boy
Book Jacket Designer
Booking Agent
Brand/Product Manager
Calligrapher
Caricaturist
Cartographer
Casting Director
Choir Director
Clown
Colorist
Comedian
Concert Musician
Concert Promoter
Conservator
Consumer Researcher
Contract Specialist
Cruise Entertainment Director
Dance Teacher
Debate Teacher
Designer
Docent
Documentary Researcher
Draftsperson
Drama Teacher
Emcee
English Teacher
Engraver
Equipment Designer

Event Planner
Facility Manager
Fashion Cutter
Film and Theater Producer
Film Editor
Film Production Accountant
Floral Designer
Food Stylist
Framer
Gaffer
Gallery Owner
Glassblower
Greensman
Greeting Card Illustrator
Grip
Ice Sculptor
Information Broker
Ink Chemist
Jewelry Designer
Kinetic Artist
Knitter
Lacemaker
Leather Goods Designer
Literary Agent
Lithographer
Location Scout
Magician
Make-up Artist
Make-up Effects Artist
Mechanical Animator
Media List Manager
MIDI Technician
Multimedia Designer
Muralist
Music Conductor
Music Instrument Designer
Music Producer
Music Sequencer

Musicologist
Needleworker
Painter
Party Planner
Playwright
Potter
Printmaker
Prop Creator
Prop Master
Public Information Officer
Publicist
Recording Engineer
Recording Executive
Sculptor
Set Caterer
Set Constructor
Set Dresser
Set Tutor
Sound Designer
Sound Engineer
Special Effects Designer
Special Effects Director
Special Effects Manufacturer
Speech Teacher
Stained Glass Artist
Studio Manager
Tapestry Maker
Technical Director
Technical or Scientific Illustrator
Textile Designer
Theater Director
Ticketing Agent
Tour Manager
Urban Planner
Videographer
Visual Effects Director
Wardrobe Mistress
Weaver
Woodworker

Big Question #6: are you on the right path?

You've covered a lot of ground so far. You've had a chance to discover more about your own potential and expectations. You've taken some time to explore the realities of a wide variety of career opportunities within this industry.

Now is a good time to sort through all the details and figure out what all this means to you. This process involves equal measures of input from your head and your heart. Be honest, think big, and, most of all, stay true to you.

You may be considering an occupation that requires years of advanced schooling which, from your point of view, seems an insurmountable hurdle. What do you do? Give up before you even get started? We hope not. We'd suggest that you try some creative thinking.

Big Activity #6:

are you on the right path?

Start by asking yourself if you want to pursue this particular career so badly that you're willing to do whatever it takes to make it. Then stretch your thinking a little to consider alternative routes, nontraditional career paths, and other equally meaningful occupations.

Following are some prompts to help you sort through your ideas. Simply jot down each prompt on a separate sheet of notebook paper and leave plenty of space for your responses.

Big Activity #6: **are you on the right path?**

ARE YOU ON THE RIGHT PATH?

One thing I know for sure about my future occupation is

I'd prefer to pursue a career that offers

I'd prefer to pursue a career that requires

A career option I'm now considering is

What appeals to me most about this career is

What concerns me most about this career is

Things that I still need to learn about this career include

Big Activity #6: **are you on the right path?**

ARE YOU ON THE RIGHT PATH?

Another career option I'm considering is

What appeals to me most about this career is

What concerns me most about this career is

Things that I still need to learn about this career include

Of these two career options I've named, the one that best fits most of my interests, skills, values, and work personality is because

At this point in the process, I am

❑ Pretty sure I'm on the right track

❑ Not quite sure yet but still interested in exploring some more

❑ Completely clueless about what I want to do

experiment with success

Right about now you may find it encouraging to learn that the average person changes careers five to seven times in his or her life. Plus, most college students change majors several times. Even people who are totally set on what they want to do often end up being happier doing something just a little bit different from what they first imagined.

So, whether you think you've found the ultimate answer to career happiness or you're just as confused as ever, you're in good company. The best advice for navigating these important life choices is this: Always keep the door open to new ideas.

As smart and dedicated as you may be, you just can't predict the future. Some of the most successful professionals in any imaginable field could never ever have predicted what—and how—they would be doing what they actually do today. Why? Because when they were in high school those jobs didn't even exist. It was not too long ago that there were no such things as personal computers, Internet research, digital cameras, mass e-mails, cell phones, or any of the other newfangled tools that are so critical to so many jobs today.

Keeping the door open means being open to recognizing changes in yourself as you mature and being open to changes in the way the world works. It also involves a certain willingness to learn new things and tackle new challenges.

It's easy to see how being open to change can sometimes allow you to go further in your chosen career than you ever dreamed. For instance, in almost any profession you can imagine, technology has fueled unprecedented opportunities. Those people and companies who have embraced this "new way of working" have often surpassed their original expectations of success. Just ask Bill Gates. He's now one of the world's wealthiest men thanks to a company called Microsoft that he cofounded while still a student at Harvard University.

It's a little harder to see, but being open to change can also mean that you may have to let go of your first dream and find a more appropriate one. Maybe your dream is to become a professional athlete. At this point in your life you may think that there's nothing in the world that would possibly make you happier. Maybe you're right and maybe you have the talent and persistence (and the lucky breaks) to take you all the way.

But maybe you don't. Perhaps if you opened yourself to new ideas you'd discover that the best career involves blending your interest in sports with your talent in writing to become a sports journalist or sports information director. Maybe your love of a particular sport and your interest in working with children might best be served in a coaching career. Who knows what you might achieve when you open yourself to all the possibilities?

So, whether you've settled on a career direction or you are still not sure where you want to go, there are several "next steps" to consider. In this section, you'll find three more Big Questions to help keep your career planning moving forward. These Big Questions are:

- Big Question #7: **who knows what you need to know?**
- Big Question #8: **how can you find out what a career is really like?**
- Big Question #9: **how do you know when you've made the right choice?**

Big Question #7: who knows what you need to know?

When it comes to the nitty-gritty details about what a particular job is really like, who knows what you need to know? Someone with a job like the one you want, of course. They'll have the inside scoop—important information you may never find in books or websites. So make talking to as many people as you can part of your career planning process.

Learn from them how they turned their own challenges into opportunities, how they got started, and how they made it to where they are now. Ask the questions that aren't covered in "official" resources, such as what it is really like to do their job, how they manage to do a good job and have a great life, how they learned what they needed to learn to do their job well, and the best companies or situations to start in.

A good place to start with these career chats or "informational interviews" is with people you know—or more likely, people you know who know people with jobs you find interesting. People you already know include your parents (of course), relatives, neighbors, friends' parents, people who belong to your place of worship or club, and so on.

All it takes to get the process going is gathering up all your nerve and asking these people for help. You'll find that nine and a half times out of 10, the people you encounter will be delighted to help, either by providing information about their careers or by introducing you to people they know who can help.

hints and tips for a successful interview

• TIP #1

Think about your goals for the interview, and write them down.

Be clear about what you want to know after the interview that you didn't know before it.

Remember that the questions for all personal interviews are not the same. You would probably use different questions to write a biography of the person, to evaluate him or her for a job, to do a history of the industry, or to learn about careers that might interest you.

Writing down your objectives will help you stay focused.

• TIP #2

Pay attention to how you phrase your questions.

Some questions that we ask people are "closed" questions; we are looking for a clear answer, not an elaboration. "What time does the movie start?" is a good example of a closed question.

Sometimes, when we ask a closed question, we shortchange ourselves. Think about the difference between "What times are the showings tonight?" and "Is there a 9 P.M. showing?" By asking the second question, you may not find out if there is an 8:45 or 9:30 show.

That can be frustrating. It usually seems so obvious when we ask a question that we expect a full answer. It's important to remember, though, that the person hearing the question doesn't always have the same priorities or know why the question is being asked.

The best example of this? Think of the toddler who answers the phone. When the caller asks, "Is your mom home?" the toddler says, "Yes" and promptly hangs up. Did the child answer the question? As far as he's concerned, he did a great job!

Another problem with closed questions is that they sometimes require so many follow-up questions that the person being interviewed feels like a suspect in an interrogation room.

A series of closed questions may go this way:

Q: What is your job title?
A: Assistant Producer
Q: How long have you had that title?
A: About two years.

Q: What was your title before that?
Q: How long did you have that title?
Q: What is the difference between the two jobs?
Q: What did you do before that?
Q: Where did you learn to do this job?
Q: How did you advance from one job to the next?

An alternative, "open" question invites conversation. An open-question interview might begin this way:

I understand you are an Assistant Producer. I'm really interested in what that job is all about and how you got to be at the level you are today.

Open questions often begin with words like:

Tell me about . . .
How do you feel about . . .
What was it like . . .

• TIP #3

Make the person feel comfortable answering truthfully. In general, people don't want to say things that they think will make them look bad. How to get at the truth? Be empathic, and make their answers seem "normal."

Ask a performer or artist how he or she feels about getting a bad review from the critics, and you are unlikely to hear, "It really hurts. Sometimes I just want to cry and get out of the business." Or "Critics are so stupid. They never understand what I am trying to do."

Try this approach instead: "So many people in your industry find it hard to deal with the hurt of a bad critical review. How do you handle it when that happens?"

ask the experts

You can learn a lot by interviewing people who are already successful in the types of careers you're interested in. In fact, we followed our own advice and interviewed several people who have been successful in the fields of art, entertainment, and communications to share with you here.

Before you get started on your own interview, take a few minutes to look through the results of some of ours. To make it easier for you to compare the responses of all the people we interviewed, we have presented our interviews as a panel discussion that reveals important success lessons these people have learned along the way. Each panelist is introduced on the next two pages.

Our interviewees gave us great information about things like what their jobs are really like, how they got to where they are, and even provided a bit of sage advice for people like you who are just getting started.

So Glad You Asked

In addition to the questions we asked in the interviews in this book, you might want to add some of these questions to your own interviews:

- How did your childhood interests relate to your choice of career path?
- How did you first learn about the job you have today?
- In what ways is your job different from how you expected it to be?
- Tell me about the parts of your job that you really like.
- If you could get someone to take over part of your job for you, what aspect would you most like to give up?
- If anything were possible, how would you change your job description?
- What kinds of people do you usually meet in your work?
- Walk me through the whole process of getting your type of product made and distributed. Tell me about all the people who are involved.
- Tell me about the changes you have seen in your industry over the years. What do you see as the future of the industry?
- Are there things you would do differently in your career if you could do it all over?

real people with real jobs in the arts and communications

Following are introductions to our panel of experts. Get acquainted with their backgrounds and then use their job titles to track their stories throughout the five success lessons.

Steven Bleicher

- Artist/**Professor Steven Bleicher** is a faculty member in the Graphic Design Department at the Art Institute in Fort Lauderdale, Florida, where he teachers students how to become professional artists and designers.
- **Art Director Stuart Brooks** works in San Francisco for a political consulting firm. His job is to develop creative concepts for a wide variety of image and promotional campaigns and media materials.
- **Illustrator Trish Burgio** of San Diego, California, works on projects as varied as magazine covers, theater posters, children's books, cartoon shows like *Duck Dodgers*, and commissioned projects for museums and large corporations.
- **Graphic Designer Barbara Davis-Long** has her own company in Silver Spring, Maryland. All of her work is in the specialized niche of direct response marketing, designing direct mail materials for associations, publishers, and nonprofit organizations.
- **Editor Stacey Freed** of Pittsfield, New York, did freelance work as a magazine editor for many years before she started working as a freelance editor for clients like the *Washington Post*. As a freelancer, one of her main responsibilities is finding work, which requires devoting time researching and writing query letters and hoping someone wants your skills and ideas.
- **TV Producer** and Writer **Bob Goodman** works in Los Angeles where he writes scripts for children's animated television series. He's won two Emmy Awards for his work on *Batman Beyond* and *The New Batman/Superman Adventures*.
- **Senior Photographer Jay Jennings** works for WRAL-TV/ Capitol Broadcasting in Raleigh, North Carolina. He is a television news photographer, a job involving going out on daily news assignments, shooting videotape and interviews, and producing stories for newscasts.

photo by: Stacey Liss Goodman

Bob Goodman

Jay Jennings

Mildred Lang

Lyle Welden

Joyce Wiswell

- **Public Relations (PR) Executive Lela Katzman** is president of Full Spectrum Communications in Loudenville, New York. A lot of her time involves pitching her clients' products to magazine editors and creating public relations materials such as press releases and magazine articles.
- **Party Emcee Kevin Kiernan** runs his own company, All About Parties, from Waldwick, New Jersey, although he takes his own brand of fun all over the United States.
- **Artist Mildred Lang** works in New York as a painter and is working toward a goal of exhibiting at a major New York gallery and having something in the Whitney Museum.
- **Journalist Jena McGregor** writes for a business magazine in New York. The key elements of her job are researching topics through academic studies and other reports, interviewing knowledgeable sources, and writing publishable news articles.
- Educational **Content Coordinator Traci Mosser** works in New York City on an animated educational television series about math and problem solving. She works closely with the content producer to develop Internet resources, helps write and edit a magazine for students, and prepares teacher guides and parent workshop material—all based on the show.
- **Cartoonist Ovi Nedelu** lives in Pasadena, California, where he creates characters used in animated television shows for children. He also develops ideas for new shows, often designing the entire visual world of the show.
- **Commercial Artist Doug Van De Zande** works in Raleigh, North Carolina, in a business where every day is different from the one before it. His main activities include meeting with clients, scouting locations for shoots, searching for props, conducting photo shoots, processing film in the darkroom, and producing truly wonderful photographs.
- **Writer Lyle Welden** is self-employed and works in Los Angeles and has written for television shows like *Homicide: Life On The Street*. Besides writing scripts for television shows and developing original concepts for new shows, he spends his work time meeting with executives and writers who run TV shows to pitch his ideas.
- **Managing Editor Joyce Wiswell** is employed by a publishing company in Royal Oak, Michigan. She is responsible for handling all of the editorial material (including all the written articles and cover copy) for a variety of magazines.

Success Lesson #1:

Work is a good thing when you find the right career.

- **Tell us a little about what you do now.**

Content Coordinator: I am the content coordinator for an animated series on public television. The goal of the series is to improve the math and problem-solving skills of kids in grades 3 to 5 through a math-mystery adventure cartoon. I work with the math content producer to develop print, Web, and outreach materials for students, teachers, and parents. I help write and edit a kids' magazine based on the show, teachers' guides, parent workshops, and more. I also help the producers develop content for the television series, making sure it's mathematically and educationally sound.

Journalist: My key responsibilities are coming up with story ideas that will be newsworthy and surprising. I pitch the idea to my editors, with enough research behind it to convince them it's worth writing about. If they like it, I begin calling knowledgeable sources, research the topic through academic studies and research reports, and finally, write the story and turn it in to my editors. Other times, my editors assign their story ideas and I report, research, and write them. A big part of being a journalist is checking for accuracy. Sometimes I do this myself, other times another member of our staff checks all the facts in the story. Fact-checking was more a part of my job when I was just starting out but continues to be something all reporters and writers emphasize in our work. I also do some editing: cleaning up text written by others and making sure it fits onto the page. In the past I have edited the "Letters to the Editor," the place readers use to voice their opinions about the stories we write.

Managing Editor: The main part of my job is to handle all editorial (that means all the written articles and cover copy) for a variety of magazines.

Artist: My current "job" is to achieve my goal of exhibiting at a major New York gallery and to have something in the Whitney Museum. I am painting, entering contests, winning prizes, and putting together a wonderful portfolio and résumé.

Illustrator: I am a professional painter of different jobs that include illustrating (sketching and painting ideas) for magazine covers, theater posters, large corporations, museums, children's books, and cartoon shows like *Duck Dodgers*.

Graphic Designer: I am a graphic designer in the direct mail field. Most of my time is spent at a computer designing. I work in a very specialized niche—direct response marketing. I design the

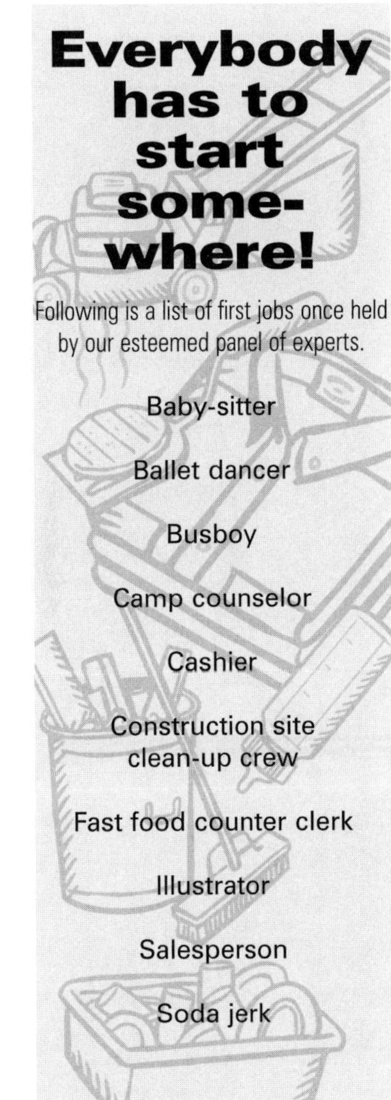

Everybody has to start some-where!

Following is a list of first jobs once held by our esteemed panel of experts.

Baby-sitter

Ballet dancer

Busboy

Camp counselor

Cashier

Construction site clean-up crew

Fast food counter clerk

Illustrator

Salesperson

Soda jerk

direct mail materials for associations, publishers, and nonprofit organizations.

Party Emcee: I emcee parties across the United States. What makes my job the best is that I get to meet great people that are planning fun and exciting events like weddings and other celebrations.

The most challenging part of running a party is to ensure that everything the client wants at the party happens. I only have four hours to do that, so I need to have really strong organizational skills. It can get tricky.

Art Director: Most of my day is spent in front of a computer, but all design concepts start with the old pencil and paper.

Commercial Artist: There is no typical day in my business. Every day is different. My job includes making appointments to show my work to prospective clients such as ad agencies, graphic designers, real estate companies, and corporations. I have to do the paperwork, which is the least fun. The main activities include location scouting for shoots, prop searching, shooting, darkroom processing and printing, meeting with clients to discuss upcoming jobs, and delivering the final product (the photo).

- **It sounds like a long way from your first job to what you do now! How did you get to this place?**

Graphic Designer: I worked in an ad agency. It was a real "trial by fire" experience.

Artist: I stopped working at other jobs in 1988, when I was 62 years old! I audited classes to open up my brain, and started drawing and painting again a few years later. I spent ten years painting and working my way through the history of art to develop my own unique style.

Writer: After I graduated from film school, I worked as a writer's assistant for five years. During that time I learned everything about putting a TV show together, from the bottom up. And I also learned a lot about what not to do when I have my own show on the air.

- **How do you get business if you're freelance or self-employed?**

Writer: A large part of my job has nothing to do with actual writing—it's meeting people and making sure that people in the position to hire me receive my writing samples and read my work. I meet executives and writers who run TV shows and sometimes pitch ideas to them. When they do hire me, they may ask me to write a script for a story they came up with or they may let me do one based on one of my original ideas for their show.

Graphic Designer: Being in the Washington, DC area, where so many associations and nonprofits are based, has been extremely helpful. I have developed a reputation among the consultants and copywriters who work with these groups.

Editor: A typical day for a freelancer includes researching and writing query letters and hoping someone wants your skills and ideas.

Commercial Artist: I've learned that doing a good job and getting along with people will lead to other contacts.

Party Emcee: The short time that I am involved in my clients' lives is usually a very important period for them. I do an excellent job, and they always remember me.

Success Lesson #2: Career ambitions change and evolve as you get older, wiser, and more experienced

- **Is this what you always wanted to do? If not, what brought you to this type of work?**

Journalist: As a child, I wanted to be a ballet dancer. Dancing was a wonderful form of expression and exercise, and I loved it. But it is difficult to go to college like a normal student and still become a dancer. I enjoyed writing and researching in college, but didn't really know what I wanted to do. I knew I wanted to do something where I would learn a little bit about a lot of different things rather than a lot about one single thing, which led me to journalism. The person who influenced me most was probably an editor of a college magazine that I worked for.

Senior Photographer: I always wanted to be someone who played professional sports or covered them as a journalist. One day I realized that I wasn't big enough, fast enough, or good enough to be an athlete, and the decision between the two became clear.

I went to journalism school at the University of Missouri intent on becoming a sportscaster. I soon realized that I wasn't cut out to be a sportscaster, but I had already fallen in love with TV photography and editing. Began my career as a TV sports photographer, and moved on to sports reporter/photographer, chief photographer, documentary photographer, and senior photographer.

Artist: I always wanted to be an artist. As a child, I was never seen without a pencil or crayon in my hand. I remember being selected to do special posters for the school in second grade and being selected in a contest for talented children sponsored by Disney.

Cartoonist: I always wanted to be an illustrator/comic/animation artist. I was passionate about getting into those fields and kept going to conventions that had anything to do with them. Eventually, I started to meet editors and producers there. I showed everyone my portfolio until I got hired.

Writer: I wanted to be the next Steven Spielberg—a writer/director of motion pictures. I am still confident that I will achieve my goal one day.

While in college, I reached a point where I could no longer afford to be a film production major. I actually had the chance to meet Steven Spielberg, and I told him my dilemma. He advised me to switch to a major in film/television writing. He said that until I could tell a story well on paper, I had no right to tell it on film. I did take his advice. Being a professional writer is a career I enjoy immensely, and I also hope to make films again, one day.

Party Emcee: In high school and college I wanted to be an attorney. I even applied to law school and was accepted. Fortunately, before I started, I realized that what I really wanted to do was to own my own business. I found this particular business through luck. I was working as a waiter when a gentleman asked to me to work for his company. I thought he was joking! And 13 years later, I'm doing exactly what I started back then, and loving it!

Content Coordinator: I always loved writing, but never thought about it as a profession until I had to write about a career in seventh grade. I wrote to a reporter at my local newspaper asking questions about her job. I don't remember any of her answers, but something definitely clicked. Then, when I was in high school, a plane crashed near my family's farm. Grabbing my camera and my notebook, I hopped on my dad's all-terrain vehicle and sped out to the action. At school the next day I showed my journalism teacher my story and pictures. We stopped the presses on our school newspaper and ran my piece on the front page. One of the city editors of our local newspaper happened to see my story as it was going through prepress and printing there. She called my journalism teacher and offered me a job at a new high school feature they were starting. That was one of the best educational career experiences I've ever had.

Success Lesson #3:
Every career has its ups and downs.

- **What do you especially like about your job?**

Senior Photographer: I love the awesome variety and the interesting people (celebrities, politicians, heroes, villains, and just plain characters). I enjoy the opportunities to travel, covering events that make history and making a real difference in the community with my work.

I met Pope John Paul II and Billy Graham, and I had the pleasure of covering 11 NCAA Final Fours.

Professor: I love being able to express myself through my art, and I love to travel and speak about art.

Journalist: The best part about the job is being able to pick up the phone and call anyone I want to because I want to try and get information from them. As part of the press, you're constantly talking to new people who teach you new things.

Editor: It's always exciting to see my name in print, especially when it's in something that I know has a lot of readers, like the *Washington Post* for which I've written a few times.

Managing Editor: My job is extremely varied, with many projects going at once. It requires attention to detail and ability to juggle many tasks. That is what I like best about it, because the time flies.

TV Producer: The best part of my job is working with other creative people. As a writer, I get to make something up out of nothing—and in doing so, I create jobs for literally hundreds of other people. And, then, I get to watch those people—actors, artists, composers, even other writers—get inspired and contribute their creativity and genius to our shared vision. It's absolutely thrilling to sit in a recording studio and hear your words performed—or in the control booth of a soundstage, and listen as a full orchestra brings your show to life with music.

Cartoonist: My job is awesome! I go to a studio and draw all day, and someone pays me for it. I design between two and five characters a day and, also, do development work for different shows.

Commercial Artist: What I like the most is the variety of work, meeting different people, and seeing how products are made. I've been to factories where auto parts are made, fabric is woven, frozen food containers are printed, and computers are assembled. I've spent a week photographing golf carts on golf courses. I have photographed candy bars, telephones, power tools, skyscrapers, fashion, annual reports, widgets that I have no idea what they do, jewelry, doctors performing knee operations, plastic fences, lumber mills, car parts. You name it, and I've probably photographed it.

Public Relations Executive: I get to communicate with a lot of different people from all over the world every day.

Content Coordinator: The best part of the job is working with a great team of people who really care about the product they are putting out; interacting with kids who love the show; and meeting celebrity voices behind the animated characters.

- **Your least favorite parts of your job?**

Art Director: Checking proofs is kind of a bummer. It's so critical that everything's perfect, and that goes against my right-brain way of working! Also, the design field is very hectic and deadline driven, so during busy periods, I kind of kiss my "real" life goodbye for a while. On the other hand, when I'm working on a design, I achieve a state where you become oblivious to time and anything outside of what you're working on. That's pretty cool!

Journalist: One of the most challenging parts of my job is writing quickly when I'm experiencing a bout of writer's block. Getting up to speed on a topic I'm not already well versed in is another challenge. That's the only downside to learning something new about so many different topics.

Senior Photographer: The worst parts are that the hours can be terrible, grueling, and unpredictable; you work when the weather's the worst; it's physically taxing work; and deadline pressure.

Content Coordinator: The worst part of my job: tough deadlines, frenetic pace.

Party Emcee: The only downside is that I often put in more than forty hours during a weekend, while most people do that in five days. You have to be committed to be successful.

Success Lesson #4: Part 1: A good education can take you places. Part 2: Formal education isn't the only way to learn.

- **How did you learn the technical skills for your job?**

Art Director: An art education background, along with openness to new experience, and a broad range of experience, especially visual. I think my fondness for travel has played a large part, being exposed to a lot of varied cultural visual input, as well as just basic quotidian life in different cultures.

Journalist: I received two college degrees, one in journalism and one in history. Both were helpful in teaching me a lot about writing and researching.

Senior Photographer: I earned a bachelor of journalism from the University of Missouri. That experience and training was and still is invaluable. There's also a wonderful network of Missouri grads throughout the country at TV networks, TV stations, newspapers, and magazines that helped me get jobs.

Commercial Artist: I landed a job with the most prestigious portrait studio in town right out of high school and three years later was accepted to Brooks Institute of Photography, one of the top photography schools in the country.

Professor: I received both my BFA and MFA from Pratt Institute. Go to the best college possible—it will pay off ten-fold.

Artist: I studied at the Art Students League in New York when I was still in high school. I went to college at Cooper Union, one of the country's finest art schools. I also took classes at the Educational Alliance in New York. At Cooper Union, I studied with people who later became famous, like Alex Katz and Hans Hoffman. They were an inspiration to me.

TV Producer: I studied film at New York University, and after college, gobbled up every course or book on writing and story structure I could find. But for years before that, I studied acting. I studied

computer science in college, too, and in my early time in filmmaking, I focused on editing. These two tasks are very similar in terms of mental activity; both helped hone my skills in logic, structure, and problem-solving—useful skills in working out a story.

- **Where else did you learn anything that helped you?**

Journalist: In college I interned for several magazines and worked for a college publication, all of which introduced me to the basics of working on the editorial staff of a magazine. I got an internship through the American Society of Magazine Editors, which helped me secure my first job in New York. I also believe my dance background taught me a great deal about time management and attention to detail. You can learn from everything you do!

Editor: Though I studied radio/TV in college, what prepared me for my career was starting at the bottom and learning as I went. I began as an editorial secretary/assistant at a magazine published by the American Society of Landscape Architects. I learned about editing from my patient boss who helped me learn and grow.

Artist: I worked at many different jobs. I did my best at each one and tried to learn as much as I could from it. I worked as a textile designer, a potter, and an administrator in charge of activities at a geriatric center.

Party Emcee: I sold copier machines when I was in college. I had to learn the core tools of selling in that job; if you did not sell, you did not make any money. My father taught me the importance of meeting new people with a handshake, look in their eyes, and remember their names.

Cartoonist: When I was in high school, I would draw after school for about six hours every day. When I went to art college, I was far ahead of the other students.

Content Coordinator: Working on MATH magazine at Scholastic has really helped in my current job.

Managing Editor: On-the-job training is essential in journalism. I highly recommend working on the school paper and getting an internship.

TV Producer: Some years ago, as a volunteer for an organization helping inner city kids, I enrolled and managed a 150-member volunteer team. That experience helped me develop leadership skills, which proved necessary as a producer, and taught me to pick up the phone and ask people for things. Believe it or not, that skill can be so daunting and is so very important!

Success Lesson #5:
Who you are influences what you do.

- **Are there personal traits that have served you especially well?**

Art Director: I think my fondness for travel has played a large part, being exposed to a lot of varied cultural visual input, as well as just basic quotidian life in different cultures.

Editor: The most important personality traits for a writer are curiosity and the need to know what happens next. And, when I worked as a waiter, I learned to get along with all types of people.

Journalist: A curious mind, a willingness to talk to anyone, and a careful attention to detail will take you very far.

Party Emcee: My ability to adapt to situations is what makes my job easier. In college I learned that waiting 'til the last minute means that you can never put 100 percent into something. You need to plan, and then attack.

Public Relations Executive: I'm very outgoing and good at small talk. I enjoy interacting with people.

Artist: I have always been independent and determined. I take initiative and do whatever I need to do.

Now it's your turn to put to work what you've learned about interviewing people with interesting jobs. Just follow the instructions for Big Activity #7.

Big Activity #7:

who knows what you need to know?

It's one thing to read about conducting an informational interview, but it's another thing altogether to actually do one. Now it's your turn to shine. Just follow these steps for doing it like a pro!

Step 1: Identify the people you want to talk to about their work.

Step 2: Set up a convenient time to meet in person or talk over the phone.

Step 3: Make up a list of questions that reflect things you'd really like to know about that person's work. Go for the open questions you just read about.

Step 4: Talk away! Take notes as your interviewee responds to each question.

Step 5: Use your notes to write up a "news" article that describes the person and his or her work.

Step 6: Place all your notes and the finished "news" article in your Big Question AnswerBook.

Big Activity #7: **who knows what you need to know?**

contact information	appointments/sample questions
name	day time
company	location
title	
address	
	sample questions:
phone	
email	
name	day time
company	location
title	
address	
	sample questions:
phone	
email	
name	day time
company	location
title	
address	
	sample questions:
phone	
email	

Big Activity #7: **who knows what you need to know?**

questions	answers
	INTERVIEW NOTES

Big Activity #7: **who knows what you need to know?**

questions	answers
	INTERVIEW NOTES

Big Activity #7: **who knows what you need to know?**

NEWS

Big Activity #7: **who knows what you need to know?**

NEWS

Big Question #8:

how can you find out what a career is really like?

There are some things you just have to figure out for yourself. Things like whether your interest in pursuing a career in marine biology is practical if you plan to live near the Mojave Desert.

Other things you have to see for yourself. Words are sometimes not enough when it comes to conveying what a job is really like on a day-to-day basis—what it looks like, sounds like, and feels like.

Here are a few ideas for conducting an on-the-job reality check.

identify typical types of workplaces

Think of all the places that jobs like the ones you like take place. Almost all of the careers in this book, or ones very similar to them, exist in the corporate world, in the public sector, and in the military. And don't forget the option of going into business for yourself!

For example: Are you interested in public relations? You can find a place for yourself in almost any sector of our economy. Of course, companies definitely want to promote their products. But don't limit yourself to the Fortune 500 corporate world. Hospitals, schools, and manufacturers need your services. Cities, states, and even countries also need your services. They want to increase tourism, get businesses to relocate there, and convince workers to live there or students to study there. Each military branch needs to recruit new members and to show how they are using the money they receive from the government for medical research, taking care of families, and other non-news-breaking uses. Charities, community organizations, and even religious groups want to promote the good things they are doing so that they will get more members, volunteers, contributions, and funding. Political candidates, parties, and special interest groups all want to promote their messages. Even actors, dancers, and writers need to promote themselves.

Not interested in public relations but know you want a career that involves lots of writing? You've thought about becoming the more obvious choices—novelist, newspaper reporter, or English teacher. But you don't want to overlook other interesting possibilities, do you?

What if you also enjoy technical challenges? Someone has to write the documentation for all those computer games and software.

Love cars? Someone has to write those owner's manuals too.

Ditto on those government reports about safety and environmental standards for industries.

Maybe community service is your thing. You can mix your love for helping people with writing grant proposals seeking funds for programs at hospitals, day care centers, or rehab centers.

Talented in art and design? Those graphics you see in magazine advertisements, on your shampoo bottle, and on a box of cereal all have to be created by someone.

That someone could be you.

find out about the job outlook

Organizations like the U.S. Bureau of Labor Statistics spend a lot of time and energy gathering data on what kinds of jobs are most in demand now and what kinds are projected to be in demand in the future. Find out what the job outlook is for a career you like. A good resource for this data can be found on-line at America's Career InfoNet at ***www.acinet.org/acinet.***

This information will help you understand whether the career options you find most appealing are viable. In other words, job outlook data will give you a better sense of your chances of actually finding gainful employment in your chosen profession—a rather important consideration from any standpoint.

Be realistic. You may really, really want to be a film critic at a major newspaper. Maybe your ambition is to become the next Roger Ebert.

Think about this. How many major newspapers are there? Is it reasonable to pin all your career hopes on a job for which there are only about 10 positions in the whole country? That doesn't mean that it's impossible to achieve your ambition. After all, someone has to fill those positions. It should just temper your plans with realism and perhaps encourage you to have a back-up plan, just in case.

look at training requirements

Understand what it takes to prepare yourself for a specific job. Some jobs require only a high school diploma. Others require a couple of years of technical training, while still others require four years or more in college.

Be sure to investigate a variety of training options. Look at training programs and colleges you may like to attend. Check out their websites to see what courses are required for the major you want. Make sure you're willing to "do the time" in school to prepare yourself for a particular occupation.

see for yourself

There's nothing quite like seeing for yourself what a job is like. Talk with a teacher or guidance counselor to arrange a job-shadowing opportunity with someone who is in the job or in a similar one.

Job shadowing is an activity that involves actually spending time at work with someone to see what a particular job is like up close and personal. It's an increasingly popular option and your school may participate in specially designated job-shadowing days. For some especially informative resources on job shadowing, visit ***www.jobshadow.org***.

Another way to test-drive different careers is to find summer jobs and internships that are similar to the career you hope to pursue.

make a Plan B

Think of the alternatives! Often it's not possible to have a full-time job in the field you love. Some jobs just don't pay enough to meet the needs of every person or family. Maybe you recognize that you don't have the talent, drive, or commitment to rise to the top. Or, perhaps you can't afford the years of work it takes to get established or you place a higher priority on spending time with family than that career might allow.

If you can see yourself in any of those categories, DO NOT GIVE UP on what you love! There is always more than one way to live out your dreams. Look at some of the other possibilities in this book. Find a way to integrate your passion into other jobs or your free time.

Lots of people manage to accomplish this in some fairly impressive ways. For instance, the Knicks City Dancers, known for their incredible performances and for pumping up the crowd at Knicks basketball games, include an environmental engineer, a TV news assignment editor, and a premed student, in addition to professional dancers. The Broadband Pickers, a North Texas bluegrass band, is made up of five lawyers and one businessman. In fact, even people who are extremely successful in a field that they love find ways to indulge their other passions. Paul Newman, the actor and director, not only drives race cars as a hobby, but also produces a line of gourmet foods and donates the profits to charity.

Get the picture? Good. Hang in there and keep moving forward in your quest to find your way toward a great future.

Big Activity #8:

how can you find out what a career is really like?

This activity will help you conduct a reality check about your future career in two ways. First, it prompts you to find out more about the nitty-gritty details you really need to know to make a well-informed career choice. Second, it helps you identify strategies for getting a firsthand look at what it's like to work in a given profession—day in and day out.

Here's how to get started:

Step 1: Write the name of the career you're considering at the top of a sheet of paper (or use the following worksheets if this is your book).

Step 2: Create a checklist (or, if this is your book, use the one provided on the following pages) covering two types of reality-check items.

First, list four types of information to investigate:

- training requirements
- typical workplaces
- job outlook
- similar occupations

Second, list three types of opportunities to pursue:

- job shadowing
- apprenticeship
- internship

Step 3: Use resources such as America's Career InfoNet at ***www. acinet. org*** and Career OneStop at ***www.careeronestop.org*** to seek out the information you need.

Step 4: Make an appointment with your school guidance counselor to discuss how to pursue hands-on opportunities to learn more about this occupation. Use the space provided on the following worksheets to jot down preliminary contact information and a brief summary of why or why not each career is right for you.

Step 5: When you're finished, place these notes in your Big Question AnswerBook.

Big Activity #8: **how can you find out what a career is really like?**

career choice:	
training requirements	
typical workplaces	
job outlook	
similar occupations	

INFORMATION

Big Activity #8: **how can you find out what a career is really like?**

job shadowing	when: where: who: observations and impressions:
apprenticeship	when: where: who: observations and impressions:
internship	when: where: who: observations and impressions:

OPPORTUNITIES

Big Question #9: how do you know when you've made the right choice?

When it comes right down to it, finding the career that's right for you is like shopping in a mall with 12,000 different stores. Finding the right fit may require trying on lots of different options.

All the Big Questions you've answered so far have been designed to expand your career horizons and help you clarify what you really want in a career. The next step is to see how well you've managed to integrate your interests, capabilities, goals, and ambitions with the realities of specific opportunities.

There are two things for you to keep in mind as you do this.

First, recognize the value of all the hard work you did to get to this point. If you've already completed the first eight activities thoughtfully and honestly, whatever choices you make will be based on solid knowledge about yourself and your options. You've learned to use a process that works just as well now, when you're trying to get an inkling of what you want to do with your life, as it will later when you have solid job offers on the table and need to make decisions that will affect your life and family.

Second, always remember that sometimes, even when you do everything right, things don't turn out the way you'd planned. That's called life. It happens. And it's not the end of the world. Even if you make what seems to be a bad choice, know this—there's no such thing as a wasted experience. The paths you take, the training you receive, the people you meet—they ultimately fall together like puzzle pieces to make you who you are and prepare you for what you're meant to do.

That said, here's a strategy to help you confirm that you are making the very best choices you can.

Big Activity #9:

how do you know when you've made the right choice?

One way to confirm that the choices you are making are right for you is to look at both sides of this proverbial coin: what you are looking for and what each career offers. The following activity will help you think this through.

Step 1: To get started, make two charts with four columns (or, if this is your book, use the following worksheets).

Step 2: Label the first column of the first chart as "Yes Please!" Under this heading list all the qualities you absolutely must have in a future job. This might include factors such as the kind of training you'd prefer to pursue (college, apprenticeship, etc.); the type of place where you'd like to work (big office, high-tech lab, in the great outdoors, etc.); and the sorts of people you want to work with (children, adults, people with certain needs, etc.). It may also include salary requirements or dress code preferences.

Step 3: Now at the top of the next three columns write the names of three careers you are considering. (This is a little like Big Activity #3 where you examined your work values. But now you know a lot more and you're ready to zero in on specific careers.)

Step 4: Go down the list and use an *X* to indicate careers that do indeed feature the desired preferences. Use an *O* to indicate those that do not.

Step 5: Tally up the number of *Xs* and *Os* at the bottom of each career column to find out which comes closest to your ideal job.

Step 6: In the first column of the second chart add a heading called "No Thanks!" This is where you'll record the factors you simply prefer not to deal with. Maybe long hours, physically demanding work, or jobs that require years of advanced training just don't cut it for you. Remember that part of figuring out what you do want to do involves understanding what you don't want to do.

Step 7: Repeat steps 2 through 5 for these avoid-at-all-costs preferences as you did for the must-have preferences above.

Big Activity #9: **how do you know when you've made the right choice?**

yes please!	career #1	career #2	career #3
totals	___X___O	___X___O	___X___O

Big Activity #9: **how do you know when you've made the right choice?**

no thanks!	career #1	career #2	career #3
totals	__X__O	__X__O	__X__O

Big Question #10: what's next?

Think of this experience as time well invested in your future. And expect it to pay off in a big way down the road. By now, you have worked (and perhaps wrestled) your way through nine important questions:

- Big Question #1: **who are you?**
- Big Question #2: **what are your interests and strengths?**
- Big Question #3: **what are your work values?**
- Big Question #4: **what is your work personality?**
- Big Question #5: **do you have the right skills?**
- Big Question #6: **are you on the right path?**
- Big Question #7: **who knows what you need to know?**
- Big Question #8: **how can you find out what a career is really like?**
- Big Question #9: **how do you know when you've made the right choice?**

But what if you still don't have a clue about what you want to do with your life?

Don't worry. You're talking about one of the biggest life decisions you'll ever make. These things take time.

It's okay if you don't have all the definitive answers yet. At least you do know how to go about finding them. The process you've used to work through this book is one that you can rely on throughout your life to help you sort through the options and make sound career decisions.

So what's next?

More discoveries, more exploration, and more experimenting with success are what come next. Keep at it and you're sure to find your way to wherever your dreams and ambitions lead you.

And, just for good measure, here's one more Big Activity to help point you in the right direction.

Big Activity #10:
what's next?

List five things you can do to move forward in your career planning process (use a separate sheet if you need to). Your list may include tasks such as talking to your guidance counselor about resources your school makes available, checking out colleges or other types of training programs that can prepare you for your life's work, or finding out about job-shadowing or internship opportunities in your community. Remember to include any appropriate suggestions from the Get Started Now! list included with each career profile in Section 2 of this book.

Big Activity #10: **what's next?**

a final word

You are now officially equipped with the tools you need to track down a personally appropriate profession any time you have the need or desire. You've discovered more about who you are and what you want. You've explored a variety of career options within a very important industry. You've even taken it upon yourself to experiment with what it might be like to actually work in certain occupations.

Now it's up to you to put all this newfound knowledge to work for you. While you're at it, here's one more thing to keep in mind: Always remember that there's no such thing as a wasted experience. Certainly some experiences are more positive than others, but they all teach us something.

Chances are you may not get everything right the first time out. It may turn out that you were incorrect about how much you would love to go to a certain college or pursue a particular profession. That doesn't mean you're doomed to failure. It simply means that you've lived and learned. Sometimes you just won't know for sure about one direction or another until you try things out a bit. Nothing about your future has to be written in stone. Allow yourself some freedom to experiment with various options until you find something that really clicks for you.

Figuring out what you want to do with the rest of your life is a big deal. It's probably one of the most exciting and among the most intimidating decisions you'll ever make. It's a decision that warrants clear-headed thought and wholehearted investigation. It's a process that's likely to take you places you never dared imagine if you open yourself up to all the possibilities. Take a chance on yourself and seek out and follow your most valued hopes and dreams into the workplace.

Best wishes for a bright future!

Appendix

a virtual support team

As you continue your quest to determine just what it is you want to do with your life, you'll find that you are not alone. There are many people and organizations who want to help you succeed. Here are two words of advice—let them! Take advantage of all the wonderful resources so readily available to you.

The first place to start is your school's guidance center. There you are quite likely to find a variety of free resources which include information about careers, colleges, and other types of training opportunities; details about interesting events, job shadowing activities, and internship options; and access to useful career assessment tools.

In addition, since you are the very first generation on the face of the earth to have access to a world of information just the click of a mouse away—use it! The following Internet resources provide all kinds of information and ideas that can help you find your future.

make an informed choice

Following are five of the very best career-oriented websites currently on-line. Be sure to bookmark these websites and visit them often as you consider various career options.

America's Career Info Net ***www.acinet.org/acinet/default.asp***

Quite possibly the most comprehensive source of career exploration anywhere, this U.S. Department of Labor website includes all kinds of current information about wages, market conditions, employers, and employment trends. Make sure to visit the site's career video library where you'll find links to over 450 videos featuring real people doing real jobs.

Careers & Colleges ***www.careersandcolleges.com***

Each year Careers & Colleges publishes four editions of *Careers & Colleges* magazine, designed to help high school students set and meet their academic, career, and financial goals. Ask your guidance counselor about receiving free copies. You'll also want to visit the excellent Careers and Colleges website. Here you'll encounter their "Virtual Guidance Counselor," an interactive career database that allows you to match your interests with college majors or careers that are right for you.

Career Voyages ***www.careervoyages.gov***

This website is brought to you compliments of collaboration between the U.S. Department of Labor and the U.S. Department of Education and is designed especially for students like you. Here you'll find information on high-growth, high-demand occupations and the skills and education needed to attain those jobs.

Job Shadow ***www.jobshadow.org***
See your future via a variety of on-line virtual job-shadowing videos and interviews featuring people with fascinating jobs.

My Cool Career ***www.mycoolcareer.com***
This website touts itself as the "coolest career dream site for teens and 20's." See for yourself as you work your way through a variety of useful self-assessment quizzes, listen to an assortment of on-line career shows, and explore all kinds of career resources.

investigate local opportunities

To get a better understanding of employment happenings in your state, visit these state-specific career information websites.

Alabama
www.ajb.org/al
www.al.plusjobs.com

Alaska
www.jobs.state.ak.us
www.akcis.org/default.htm

Arizona
www.ajb.org/az
www.ade.state.az.us/cte/AZCrnproject10.asp

Arkansas
www.ajb.org/ar
www.careerwatch.org
www.ioscar.org/ar

California
www.calmis.ca.gov
www.ajb.org/ca
www.eurekanet.org

Colorado
www.coloradocareer.net
www.coworkforce.com/lmi

Connecticut
www1.ctdol.state.ct.us/jcc
www.ctdol.state.ct.us/lmi

Delaware
www.ajb.org/de
www.delewareworks.com

District of Columbia
www.ajb.org/dc
www.dcnetworks.org

Florida
www.Florida.access.bridges.com
www.employflorida.net

Georgia
www.gcic.peachnet.edu
(Ask your school guidance counselor for your school's free password and access code)
www.dol.state.ga.us/js

Hawaii
www.ajb.org/hi
www.careerkokua.org

Idaho
www.ajb.org/id
www.cis.idaho.gov

Illinois
www.ajb.org/il
www.ilworkinfo.com

Indiana
www.ajb.org/in
http://icpac.indiana.edu

Iowa
www.ajb.org/ia
www.state.ia.us/iccor

Kansas
www.ajb.org/ks
www.kansasjoblink.com/ada

Kentucky
www.ajb.org/ky

Louisiana
www.ajb.org/la
www.ldol.state.la.us/jobpage.asp

Maine
www.ajb.org/me
www.maine.gov/labor/lmis

Maryland
www.ajb.org/md
www.careernet.state.md.us

Massachusetts
www.ajb.org/ma
http://masscis.intocareers.org

Michigan
www.mois.org

Minnesota
www.ajb.org/mn
www.iseek.org

Mississippi
www.ajb.org/ms
www.mscareernet.org

Missouri
www.ajb.org/mo
www.greathires.org

Montana
www.ajb.org/mt
http://jsd.dli.state.mt.us/mjshome.asp

Nebraska
www.ajb.org/ne
www.careerlink.org

New Hampshire
www.nhes.state.nh.us

New Jersey
www.ajb.org/nj
www.wnjpin.net/coei

New Mexico
www.ajb.org/nm
www.dol.state.nm.us/soicc/upto21.html

Nevada
www.ajb.org/nv
http://nvcis.intocareers.org

New York
www.ajb.org/ny
www.nycareerzone.org

North Carolina
www.ajb.org/nc
www.ncsoicc.org
www.nccareers.org

North Dakota
www.ajb.org/nd
www.imaginend.com
www.ndcrn.com/students

Ohio
www.ajb.org/oh
https://scoti.ohio.gov/scoti_lexs

Oklahoma
www.ajb.org/ok
www.okcareertech.org/guidance
http://okcrn.org

Oregon
www.hsd.k12.or.us/crls

Pennsylvania
www.ajb.org/pa
www.pacareerlink.state.pa.us

Rhode Island
www.ajb.org/ri
www.dlt.ri.gov/lmi/jobseeker.htm

South Carolina
www.ajb.org/sc
www.scois.org/students.htm

South Dakota
www.ajb.org/sd

Tennessee
www.ajb.org/tn
www.tcids.utk.edu

Texas
www.ajb.org/tx
www.ioscar.org/tx
www.cdr.state.tx.us/Hotline/Hotline.html

Utah
www.ajb.org/ut
http://jobs.utah.gov/wi/occi.asp

Vermont
www.ajb.org/vt
www.vermontjoblink.com
www.vtlmi.info/oic.cfm

Virginia
www.ajb.org/va
www.vacrn.net

Washington
www.ajb.org/wa
www.workforceexplorer.com
www.wa.gov/esd/lmea/soicc/sohome.htm

West Virginia
www.ajb.org/wv
www.state.wv.us/bep/lmi

Wisconsin
www.ajb.org/wi
www.careers4wi.wisc.edu
http://wiscareers.wisc.edu/splash.asp

Wyoming
www.ajb.org/wy
http://uwadmnweb.uwyo.edu/SEO/wcis.htm

get a job

Whether you're curious about the kinds of jobs currently in big demand or you're actually looking for a job, the following websites are a great place to do some virtual job-hunting.

America's Job Bank *www.ajb.org*

Another example of your (or, more accurately, your parent's) tax dollars at work, this well-organized website is sponsored by the U.S. Department of Labor. Job seekers can post resumes and use the site's search engines to search through over a million job listings by location or by job type.

Monster.com *www.monster.com*

One of the Internet's most widely used employment websites, this is where you can search for specific types of jobs in specific parts of the country, network with millions of people, and find useful career advice.

explore by special interests

An especially effective way to explore career options is to look at careers associated with a personal interest or fascination with a certain type of industry. The following websites help you narrow down your options in a focused way.

What Interests You? ***www.bls.gov/k12***

This Bureau of Labor Statistics website provides information about careers associated with 12 special interest areas: math, reading, science, social studies, music and arts, building and fixing things, helping people, computers, law, managing money, sports, and nature.

Construct My Future ***www.constructmyfuture.com***

With over $600 billion annually devoted to new construction projects, about 6 million Americans build careers in this industry. This website, sponsored by the Association of Equipment Distributors, the Association of Equipment Manufacturers, and Associated General Contractors, introduces an interesting array of construction-related professions.

Dream It Do It ***www.dreamit-doit.com***

In order to make manufacturing a preferred career choice by 2010, the National Association of Manufacturing's Center for Workforce Success is reaching out to young adults and their parents, educators, communities, and policy-makers to change their minds about manufacturing's future and its careers. This website introduces high-demand 21st-century manufacturing professions many will find surprising and worthy of serious consideration.

Get Tech ***www.gettech.org***

Another award-winning website from the National Association of Manufacturing.

Take Another Look ***www.Nrf.com/content/foundation/rcp/main.htm***

The National Retail Federation challenges students to take another look at their industry by introducing a wide variety of careers associated with marketing and advertising, store management, sales, distribution and logistics, e-commerce, and more.

Index

Page numbers in **boldface** indicate main articles. Page numbers in *italics* indicate photographs.

A

T

U